Building English Skills

**Red Level
Canadian Edition**

Skills Practice Book

Skills Practice Books

Purple Level

Yellow Level

Blue Level

Orange Level

Green Level

RED LEVEL

Gold Level

Silver Level

Aqua Level

Brown Level

The Book Society of Canada Limited
Agincourt   Canada

Special Features of This Skills Practice Book

- It contains thousands of skill-building exercises in composition, vocabulary, grammar, usage, capitalization, punctuation, and spelling.

- Each page is a self-contained unit. It contains a brief explanation, followed by an average of twenty reinforcing exercises.

- Each page focuses on one—and only one—topic or skill.

- Key words and phrases are printed in color for greater clarity and ease of use.

- A comprehensive review lesson follows each major section of the text.

This Canadian edition prepared by the Staff of The Book Society of Canada Limited is derived from the Skills Practice Book conceived and developed by the Staff of McDougal, Littell & Company.

Canadian Cataloguing in Publication Data

Main entry under title:
Skills practice book, red level

(Building English skills)
For use in grade 7.
ISBN 0-7725-5136-7

1. English language — Composition and exercises.
I. Series.

LB1576.S64   428.2   C82-095234-6

ISBN 0-7725-5136-7 (Student's)

ISBN 0-7725-5137-5 (Teacher's)

Copyright © 1982 by McDougal, Littell & Company
This edition Copyright © 1983, The Book Society of Canada Limited

1 2 3 4 5 6 7 8 JD 90 89 88 87 86 85 84 83
Printed and bound in Canada by John Deyell Company

Contents

Composition

Grammar, Usage, and Mechanics

The Sentence and Its Parts

Using Verbs

Using Nouns

Using Pronouns

Composition

English and Its Relatives

Linguists—people who study language—saw long ago that some languages are related. They noticed that words in some languages were like words in some other languages. These likenesses still show among English and some of its relatives. This chart shows four words in English and in four related languages.

ENGLISH	FRENCH	SPANISH	ITALIAN	GERMAN
swim	nager	nadar	nuotare	schwimmen
man	homme	hombre	uomo	Mann
sleep	dormir	dormir	dormire	schlafen
speak	parler	hablar	parlare	sprechen

Judging from the chart, what language do you think seems to be the closest relative of English? _____

The following chart is incomplete. It shows words in French, Spanish, Italian, and German only. The related English words are missing. Write in the related English words. They are listed at the bottom of the page.

	ENGLISH	FRENCH	SPANISH	ITALIAN	GERMAN
1.	_____	aider	ayudar	aiutare	helfen
2.	_____	avoir	haber	avere	haben
3.	_____	lait	leche	latte	Milch
4.	_____	étoile	estrella	stella	Stern
5.	_____	vivre	vivir	vìvere	leben
6.	_____	mourir	morir	morire	sterben
7.	_____	montagne	montaña	montagna	Berg
8.	_____	hiver	invierno	invèrno	Winter
9.	_____	printemps	primavera	primavera	Frühling
10.	_____	viande	carne	carne	Fleisch
11.	_____	soleil	sol	sole	Sonne
12.	_____	lune	luna	luna	Mond
13.	_____	terre	tierra	tèrra	Erde
14.	_____	air	aire	ària	Luft
15.	_____	rouge	rojo	rosso	rot

RELATED ENGLISH WORDS: star, winter, moon, have, die, red, meat, air, earth, sun, spring, mountain, live, milk, help

Anglo-Saxon Words

In about A.D. 550, Anglo-Saxon tribes that had been living in northern Europe succeeded in conquering Britain. These tribes spoke one of the West Germanic languages that was used in that part of Europe. Linguists call their language **Anglo-Saxon.** We can think of Anglo-Saxon as the beginning of the English we speak today. Some Anglo-Saxon words are still in use. They are small but important words that we use very often. They haven't changed much since the Anglo-Saxons brought them to Britain.

See how many Anglo-Saxon words you can recognize in modern English. Match the Anglo-Saxon words in the left column with the modern English words in the right column. Write each Anglo-Saxon word on the line following the modern English word that matches it.

bringan	1. word _____
cald	2. through _____
docga	3. cold _____
waeter	4. before _____
word	5. water _____
gecnawan	6. go _____
thurh	7. write _____
baec	8. bring _____
mycel	9. back _____
beforan	10. dog _____
gan	11. know _____
god	12. why _____
writan	13. look _____
hwi	14. much _____
locian	15. good _____
thencan	16. must _____
moste	17. old _____
tacan	18. right _____
reht	19. think _____
eald	20. take _____

How New Words Are Added to Our Language (I)

The making of new English words goes on and on. One way for speakers of English to make new words is to borrow words from other languages. However, there are other ways to create new words.

Putting two words together makes a new **compound word.**

book + shelf = bookshelf   motor + cycle = motorcycle

Putting only parts of two words together makes a new word called a **blend.**

smoke + fog = smog   squirm + wiggle = squiggle

Cutting off part of a word and using only the short form makes a new word called a **clipped word.**

gymnasium—gym   examination—exam

Making a new word from initials creates a word called an **acronym.**

sound **n**avigation **a**nd **r**anging = sonar

United **N**ations **I**nternational **C**hildren's **E**mergency **F**und = UNICEF

Label each of the italicized words to show whether it is a **compound,** a **blend,** a **clipped word,** or an **acronym.** Then, on the line following each word, tell what word or words it has been made from. Use a dictionary for help.

1. _____ *radar* _____

2. _____ *greenhouse* _____

3. _____ *stereo tapes* _____

4. _____ *plane* _____

5. _____ *prop plane* _____

6. _____ *laser* _____

7. _____ *scrapbook* _____

8. _____ *moped* _____

9. _____ *ref* _____

10. _____ *brunch* _____

11. _____ *Skylab* _____

12. _____ *pop music* _____

13. _____ *feedback* _____

14. _____ *flu* _____

15. _____ *ad* _____

How New Words Are Added to Our Language (II)

4

Many words in English have come from the names of people or places that have become widely known. A. M. Ampère, for example, was a French physicist who studied electricity. Today, a measure of the strength of an electric current is called an ampere or an amp. If you look at an electric fuse, you will find that it has a rating in amps. If you look at an electric light bulb, you will find a rating given in watts. This term comes from the name of James Watt, a Scottish engineer who is best known for his work on the steam engine.

Answer each of the following with a word from a name.

1. Amelia J. Bloomer was an American feminist who lived in the nineteenth century. She urged women to get more exercise. She suggested they give up long skirts and wear loose fitting pants that would allow them to be more active. This outfit came to be called _____.

2. In 1880, Captain C. C. Boycott, an Irish landowner, raised the rents on his property. People were so upset that they refused to have anything to do with him. Today when people band together and refuse to trade with a company or country, we call it a _____.

3. The Roman goddess of agriculture was Ceres. Our name for grains and for the breakfast foods made from them is _____.

4. In the seventeenth century, Thomas Derrick was a famous London hangman. Today the name for a tall framework, like the framework around an oil well, is a _____.

5. While Mr. Derrick was going about his business, a London shopkeeper named Doily was going about his. He sold, among other things, little mats to put under vases so that they wouldn't scratch a table. Today a little mat like that is called a _____.

Review: The Story of Our Language   5

Identifying English Words. Try to match these Anglo-Saxon words and borrowed words with their English equivalents. Choose from the words at the bottom of the exercise.

1. daeg _____

2. strada _____

3. ideia _____

4. witan _____

5. fleur _____

6. haebbe _____

7. sceo _____

8. sprechen _____

9. laghe _____

10. sonne _____

WORDS: day, idea, have, law, sun, street, witty, flower, sky, speak

Adding Words to Our Language. Tell how each of the following words was added to our language. Choose from **compound, blend, clipped word, acronym,** or **word from name.**

Example: OPEC _*acronym*_____

1. fingerprint _____

2. chortle _____

3. bowie knife _____

4. taxi _____

5. sonar _____

6. tablecloth _____

7. birdhouse _____

8. exam _____

9. splatter _____

10. NATO _____

Root Words

An important way to enlarge our language is to add different beginnings and endings to a **root word.** The root word is the part of the word that contains the basic meaning.

ROOT WORD: connect   disconnect
                                  connection
                                  unconnected

In the example, the root word is judge and all the other words are formed by adding a beginning, an ending, or both, to it.

Finding the Root Words. Find the root word in each of the following examples. Write the root word on the blank. Watch your spelling.

1. unable _____
2. prejudge _____
3. worker _____
4. placement _____
5. freedom _____
6. famous _____
7. breakable _____
8. reread _____
9. baker _____
10. opposition _____
11. unreasonable _____
12. nonsense _____
13. pretest _____
14. careful _____
15. friendly _____
16. renew _____
17. confession _____
18. measurement _____
19. talkative _____
20. submarine _____
21. operator _____
22. lucky _____
23. untie _____
24. mislead _____
25. happily _____
26. wandering _____
27. unreal _____
28. irregular _____
29. rejoin _____
30. poisonous _____

Prefixes (I)

A **prefix** is a word part added at the beginning of a word. When a prefix is added, it changes the meaning of the word. It creates a new word.

PREFIX   ROOT WORD

mis   +   spell   = misspell

Here are five frequently used prefixes.

mis-   This prefix always means "wrong." To *misspell* a word is to give the wrong spelling.

non-   The meaning is always "not." A *nonconformist* is someone who does not conform.

pre-   The prefix *pre-* always means "before." *Precede* means "go before."

un-   There are two meanings for this prefix. It may mean "not" as in *unashamed*. It may also mean "the opposite of" as in *undo*.

dis-   The meaning may be "the opposite of" or "away." The opposite of *comfort* is *discomfort*. To *dismiss* someone is to send that person away.

Using Prefixes. Use any of the prefixes on the left with any of the root words on the right. Make as many new words as you can.

mis-	cover	_____	_____
dis-	place	_____	_____
non-	color	_____	_____
pre-	historic	_____	_____
un-	paid	_____	_____

Learning the Meaning of Prefixes. Complete the following sentences.

1. If a person who is *popular* is well liked, a person who is *unpopular* is

_____.

2. When you *embark*, you go aboard or begin; when you *disembark*, you

_____.

3. If something is *prearranged*, it is _____.

4. An organization for *profit* makes money; a *nonprofit* organization

_____.

5. In the paper there was a *misprint*. This means it was _____

_____.

Prefixes (II)

Here are some other prefixes.

sub- This prefix may mean "under" or "less than." A *submarine* is a ship that goes under the water.

super- The prefix *super-* may mean "above" or "more than." *Superfine* means "more than fine."

re- This prefix may mean "back" or "again." If you *rewrite* a paper, you write it again. When you have a *relapse*, you go back to a former state.

in- This prefix may also be spelled *im-*, *ir-*, or *il-*. It may mean "not" as in *impractical*. The prefix may also mean "in" as in *immigrate*, to come into a new country.

There are some words that look as if they have prefixes but really don't. The *un-* in *union* is not a prefix but part of the root word. Try to decide if the word makes sense when you think of the meaning of the prefix. Does "not ion" make sense? No. Then *un-* in *union* is not a prefix.

Finding Prefixes. Some of the words listed below have prefixes, and some don't. Circle each word that has a prefix, and underline the prefix.

Example: (impatient)

1. indirect
2. read
3. supermarket
4. subway
5. region

6. superb
7. irresistible
8. inexpensive
9. inch
10. refill

Learning the Meaning of Prefixes. Complete the following sentences.

1. If *soil* is surface dirt, then *subsoil* is _____.

2. If you have *input* in a decision, you _____.

3. Mary thought about, or *considered*, an idea; then she *reconsidered* it or _____.

4. Regular humans have normal powers; someone who is *superhuman* is

_____.

5. Something *practical* is useful; something *impractical* is _____.

Suffixes (I)

A **suffix** is a word part added at the end of a word. Like a prefix, a suffix changes the meaning of the word.

home + less = homeless (without a home)

Study the following suffixes.

-er (or **-or**) "a person or thing that does something." A *worker* is a person who works.

-fold "so many times as much." *Fivefold* is five times as much.

-ward "in the direction of." *Eastward* is in the direction of east.

-less "without." *Friendless* is without a friend.

Using Suffixes. Underline the suffix in each word below. Then write the root word in the blank. Watch your spelling.

ROOT WORD	ROOT WORD
1. actor _____	11. endless _____
2. sevenfold _____	12. tenfold _____
3. creator _____	13. upward _____
4. westward _____	14. user _____
5. fearless _____	15. ninefold _____
6. printer _____	16. countless _____
7. laborer _____	17. governor _____
8. pointless _____	18. frontward _____
9. backward _____	19. toothless _____
10. dreamer _____	20. fastener _____

Suffixes (II)

Here are some other frequently used suffixes.

-able (or **-ible**)   "can be" or "having this quality." Something that is *wash-able* can be washed without damage. A *peaceable* person is one who has the quality of peace.

-ful   "full of" or "having." A *careful* person is full of care.

-ous   "full of" or "having." A *gracious* person is one having grace.

When a suffix is added to a root word, a letter may be changed or dropped or doubled.

grace + ous = gracious   decode + er = decoder   win + er = winner

Using Suffixes. Underline the suffix in each word below. Then write the meaning of the whole word on the blank.

1. comfortable _____

2. cheerful _____

3. joyous _____

4. famous _____

5. obtainable _____

6. thoughtful _____

7. thunderous _____

8. handful _____

9. harmful _____

10. fashionable _____

Spelling with Suffixes. Put the following root words and suffixes together. Check the spelling in a dictionary if necessary.

1. love + able = _____

2. bat + er = _____

3. mercy + ful = _____

4. supply + er = _____

5. cure + able = _____

6. glory + ous = _____

7. glamor +ous = _____

8. two + fold = _____

9. beauty + ful = _____

10. employ + er = _____

Using the Dictionary

A good dictionary is the best source of information about words. It tells about the meanings and spellings of words.

The words in a dictionary are arranged in alphabetical order. You will find words more easily if you learn to open the dictionary at the right spot.

If two words have the same first letter, they are alphabetized by the second letter. If the second letter is the same, then the third letter determines which word is first. The following sets of words are in alphabetical order.

bay	change	field	pliers
block	channel	fifteen	plod

Alphabetizing Words. Alphabetize each separate group of words.

1. liquid _____
2. predict _____
3. chalk _____
4. about _____
5. thing _____
6. chance _____
7. effort _____
8. urge _____
9. linger _____
10. there _____

1. within _____
2. motor _____
3. zipper _____
4. fabric _____
5. earth _____
6. zither _____
7. invade _____
8. latter _____
9. jam _____
10. invite _____

At the top of each page in the dictionary you will find **guide words.** The guide word at the top left of the page is the first word on that page. The guide word at the top right is the last word on the page. The other words on the page fall between the two guide words.

Using Guide Words. List the following words in alphabetical order under the correct set of guide words.

cure, cube, curfew, cucumber, cupful, cultivate, curb, cup, cuff, cuddle

cub	**cumber**
1. _____
2. _____
3. _____
4. _____
5. _____

Cumberland	**curious**
1. _____
2. _____
3. _____
4. _____
5. _____

The Many Meanings of Words (I)   **12**

Most words in English have more than one meaning. When you look up a word to find its meaning, you must be sure to find the right meaning for what you are reading. Look at the dictionary entry for *book* from *Webster's New World Dictionary* (Students Edition), 1976.

Dictionary Entry for *Book*

book (book) **n.** [OE. *boc*, pl. *bec*, akin to OE. *bece*, BEECH < IE. base *bhago-s*, beech: runes were first carved on beech tablets] **1.** *a)* a number of sheets of paper, etc. with writing or printing on them, fastened together along one edge, usually between protective covers *b)* a relatively long piece of writing, as a novel, history, scientific work, etc. **2.** a main division of a literary work **3.** *a)* a number of blank or ruled sheets or printed forms bound together [an account *book*] *b)* a record or account kept in this **4.** the words of an opera, musical play, etc.; libretto **5.** a booklike package, as of matches or tickets **6.** a record of bets, as on horse races **7.** *Bridge*, etc. a specified number of tricks that must be won before scoring can take place —**vt.** **1.** to record in a book; list **2.** to engage (rooms, performers, etc.) ahead of time [to *book* passage on a ship] **3.** to record charges against on a police record [he was *booked* for driving while drunk] —**adj.** in, from, or according to books or accounts —**bring to book** to force to explain —**by the book** according to the rules —**close the books** *Bookkeeping* to make no further entries —**in one's book** in one's opinion —**keep books** to keep a record of business transactions —**know like a book** to know well or fully —☆**make book** [Slang] to make or accept bets —☆**one for the books** [Colloq.] something very surprising, unexpected, etc. —**on the books** **1.** recorded **2.** enrolled —**the Book** the Bible —☆**throw the book at** [Slang] **1.** to place all possible charges against (an accused person) **2.** to give the maximum punishment to —**book′er n.**

Finding the Meanings of Words. For each of the following sentences, write the specific meaning of *book* that applies.

1. Do you collect match *books?* _____

2. The accountant kept a set of *books* for every client. _____

3. Roland's *book* of biology notes was nearly complete. _____

4. Six tricks in bridge make a *book.* _____

5. She lived *by the book.* _____

6. The officer *booked* the driver for leaving the scene of the accident.

_____

7. Have you read the *book Little Women?* _____

8. The corporation *closed its books* for inventory. _____

9. Our pastor quoted from the *Book of Matthew.* _____

10. The Schubert Theater has *booked* the Ace Trucking Company for

six performances. _____

The Many Meanings of Words (II) 13

A good way to develop your vocabulary and be more exact in your written and spoken language is to learn the many meanings of words.

Working with Word Meanings. The word *meet* can be used in many different ways. For each of the sentences below, tell the meaning of the word as it is used in that particular sentence. Use a dictionary if necessary.

1. Jean and Julia will *meet* my train.

_____

2. Did you *meet* the new student in Mr. Lowe's class?

_____

3. Stevenson High had a track *meet* yesterday.

_____

4. The executives of the company will *meet* to discuss the problem.

_____

5. The French troops will *meet* the enemy on the battlefield.

_____

Using Different Word Meanings. The word *play* has many meanings. Write five sentences, each using a different meaning of the word *play*. Each sentence should clearly show the meaning of the word. Use a dictionary if necessary.

1. _____

_____

2. _____

_____

3. _____

_____

4. _____

_____

5. _____

_____

Synonyms (I)

Words that are very close to each other in meaning are called **synonyms**. Following is a list of synonyms for *say*.

say: assert, state, declare, express, speak, talk, utter, pronounce, recite

All of these words have meanings like *say*, but they are not exactly like *say*. If you want to *say* something very positively, you might *assert* it. If you were going to *say* a poem, you would *recite* the poem, not *assert* it.

There are many words that are already a part of your vocabulary that may be overworked and may need help from other words. For example, the word *interesting* could be replaced by such words as *exciting, alluring, fascinating,* or *curious.* Each word may give a more exact idea of what you are trying to say.

Using Synonyms. Following is a list of synonyms for **beat.** These might be used in sports headlines. Below the list of synonyms is a list of hockey scores. Write a headline for each game. Choose a word that fits the score.

thrash	blast	top	hammer
edge	clobber	nip	trounce
pound	smash	slaughter	crush

1. Oilers 5, Islanders 1 _____

2. Rangers 4, Maple Leafs 2 _____

3. Red Wings 1, Sabres 0 _____

4. Canucks 3, Flyers 2 _____

5. Nordiques 4, Black Hawks 1 _____

Choosing a Better Word. Underline the more exact word in each of the following sentences.

1. A (cold, piercing) wind lashed at me as I made my way up the street.

2. I have never seen anything as (bad, dreadful) as that accident.

3. Tom (guffawed, giggled) heartily at his mistake.

4. It was such a beautiful summer day that we (strolled, marched) through the park.

5. We (pulled, tugged) at the rope with all our might.

Synonyms (II)

If you are going to describe something, take time to think about the words you will use. Have you picked the word that best describes what you have in mind? Is there a word that comes closer to what you want to say? What kind of word will describe the mood you want to create?

Using Synonyms. List as many synonyms as you can for each of the italicized words in the following phrases.

1. a *nice* day _____

2. a *big* city _____

3. a *bright* fire _____

4. an *unusual* thing _____

5. a *funny* cartoon _____

6. the *right* answer _____

7. a *bad* smell _____

8. a *hard* assignment _____

9. a *weak* opponent _____

10. my *shy* friend _____

Rewriting Sentences Using Synonyms. Rewrite each of the following sentences, creating a better word picture. Use synonyms for the words in italics.

1. The woman *walked* down the *street*.

_____

2. My mother *said,* "I'm so *glad* you could come."

_____

3. The news story *scared* the townspeople.

_____

4. Our basketball team *beat* the visiting team easily.

_____

5. The chipmunks *ran* through the underbrush.

_____

Antonyms

Words that are opposite or nearly opposite to each other in meaning are called **antonyms.** The words *big* and *little* are antonyms, and so are *hot* and *cold*.

Antonyms can be useful when you want to compare things. You might say that the new office building was so *enormous* that the apartment house next door looked *tiny* by comparison.

Using Antonyms. Write an antonym for each of the following words.

1. difficult _____   6. like _____

2. soft _____   7. above _____

3. always _____   8. hopeful _____

4. pretty _____   9. smooth _____

5. arrive _____   10. brave _____

Using Antonyms. For each sentence below, write another sentence, using the antonym of the italicized word.

1. An *honest* person does not cheat or steal.

_____

2. I was *busy* all day.

_____

3. We saw a *taped* television show.

_____

4. The *light* gray coat showed every stain.

_____

5. A diamond ring is very *expensive*.

_____

Review: Building Your Vocabulary

Using Root Words, Prefixes, and Suffixes. Add a prefix or a suffix or both to each root word below. Write the word and its meaning on the blank.

mis-, non-, pre-, un-, dis-, sub-, super-, re-, in-
-er, -or, -fold, -ward, -less, -able, -ful, -ous

Example: spell *misspell - to give the wrong spelling*

1. rule _____

2. certain _____

3. locate _____

4. human _____

5. humor _____

6. sense _____

7. reason _____

8. divide _____

9. five _____

10. south _____

11. charge _____

12. care _____

Using Synonyms and Antonyms. Give a synonym and an antonym for each of the following words.

	SYNONYM	ANTONYM
1. friend	_____	_____
2. odd	_____	_____
3. cold	_____	_____
4. quick	_____	_____
5. good	_____	_____
6. happy	_____	_____
7. start	_____	_____
8. bad	_____	_____

The Sense of Sight

You can see everything around you, but do you ever stop to examine something carefully enough so that you can describe it precisely?

Here are two descriptions of the same scene. Which one helps the reader "see" better?

> The man stood in the forest. He was looking for something. He saw nothing.

> The wiry young man stood in the midst of lush greenery, looking intently for a flash of color among the trees. All he saw was green.

Try to use "sight" words in your writing. Make your descriptions vivid and colorful. Create a word picture for your reader.

Here are some "sight" words you might use:

COLOR	MOVEMENT	SHAPE	APPEARANCE
beige	scamper	crinkled	glimmering
olive	dash	portly	messy
coral	crawl	wiry	cluttered
plum	saunter	square	muddy
coffee	shiver	thin	massive

Using "Sight" Words. Describe the following situations as vividly as you can. Try to create word pictures, painting with words. Use words of color, movement, shape, and appearance.

1. your backyard in summer _____

_____

_____

_____

2. a surprise party _____

_____

_____

_____

3. your favorite animal _____

_____

_____

_____

The Sense of Hearing

Most of us hear well enough, but we don't listen. Can you hear all the sounds that surround you? Can you hear silence? Think about each sound separately.

There are many words that describe the sounds you hear.

LOUD SOUNDS	SOFT SOUNDS	SPEECH SOUNDS
crash	sigh	giggle
thunder	murmur	sing
racket	snap	snort
yell	patter	chatter
blare	swish	drawl

Using "Hearing" Words in Your Writing. Here are sounds you are familiar with. Write a sentence about each sound, describing it as vividly as you can.

1. a car starting on a cold morning _____

_____

2. the noise at a hockey game _____

_____

3. a circus _____

_____

4. a fire _____

_____

5. a snake in the grass _____

_____

6. water in a stream _____

_____

7. a group at a table at McDonald's _____

_____

8. a falling tree _____

_____

9. a telephone _____

_____

10. a classroom at night _____

_____

The Sense of Touch

Describing how things feel can often be difficult, especially when you want your reader to experience the same feeling you experienced. A good way to handle the problem is to compare something with something else.

The dry ice felt like a torch searing my hand.

Here are some "touch" words.

icy	sharp	feathery	gritty	rough
gummy	crisp	slippery	cutting	greasy
mushy	smooth	dull	piercing	brittle

Using "Touch" Words in Your Writing. Write a sentence for each of the following things, describing how each feels. Try to think of new comparisons so your reader won't lose interest.

1. a porcupine _____

_____

2. a wet towel _____

_____

3. a banana peel _____

_____

4. fur _____

_____

5. a cast on a broken arm _____

_____

6. a flower petal _____

_____

7. hitting a baseball _____

_____

8. a snowball _____

_____

9. a handshake _____

_____

10. cleaning a fish _____

_____

The Sense of Taste

There are probably many foods and drinks that you have tasted. Some were delicious; others didn't appeal to you. Have you ever tried to describe these foods and drinks to someone else?

Taste words help you describe vividly your sense of taste.

salty	nutty	buttery	burnt	sweet
spicy	raw	bland	sour	bitter
tart	hearty	lemony	rotten	juicy

Using "Taste" Words in Your Writing. Write a sentence about each of the following foods or drinks. Describe the taste as vividly as you can.

1. beef stew _____

_____

2. French dressing _____

_____

3. cola _____

_____

4. potato chips _____

_____

5. a peanut butter and jelly sandwich _____

_____

6. a peach _____

_____

7. a taffy apple _____

_____

8. cough syrup _____

_____

9. raisins _____

_____

10. cheese _____

_____

The Sense of Smell

Most people are aware of strong odors, but they are less sensitive to delicate ones. You need to make a conscious effort to be more aware of smells and to train your nose to identify them.

Here are several words to help you.

fragrant	spicy	spoiled	fresh	fishy
earthy	smoky	musty	fruity	clean
piney	burnt	damp	mildewy	medicinal

Using "Smell" Words in Your Writing. Write a sentence describing the smell of each of the following things. Try to remember exactly how each of the things smells before you write.

1. pizza _____

_____

2. the woods in spring _____

_____

3. garbage _____

_____

4. an aquarium that needs cleaning _____

_____

5. an unused basement _____

_____

6. a doctor's office _____

_____

7. a gymnasium _____

_____

8. your kitchen at suppertime _____

_____

9. a bakery _____

_____

10. a polluted pond _____

_____

Using All of the Senses

Decide which of your senses is involved in the following sentences. Write that sense **(sight, hearing, touch, taste,** or **smell)** after each sentence.

1. The chrome-trimmed car gleamed in the sunlight. _____

2. A stagnant odor came from the swamp. _____

3. We felt cool and damp as we stood near the falls. _____

4. The crowd roared at the touchdown. _____

5. Thelma bit into the spicy taco. _____

6. The faint chimes of the church bells broke the silence. _____

7. A domed object settled on the glistening snow. _____

8. Leon didn't like the bland, ripe avocado. _____

9. Roses and gardenias perfumed the air. _____

10. The leaf felt waxy on one side and furry on the other. _____

11. Sandpaper is rough and gritty. _____

12. The muscular orangutan loped through the jungle. _____

13. With a crimson face and clenched hands, Susan stalked from the room. _____

14. The savory scent of clam chowder filled the room. _____

15. Mary and Stan relished the sugary waffle. _____

16. I took a bite of the uncooked fish. _____

17. The stench of the mildewed clothes was all over. _____

18. Lithe, supple gymnasts flew over the bars. _____

19. Breezes whispered through the evergreens. _____

20. The newborn puppy felt warm and fuzzy. _____

21. We followed the tempting aroma all the way home. _____

22. We looked up to find a freckled face and toothless grin staring at us. _____

23. An earsplitting whistle pierced the air. _____

24. The smooth, fragile sculpture stood in the corner. _____

25. The seagulls swooped down like dive bombers. _____

Review: Using the Senses

In the following sentences, underline the word in each that creates the more vivid word picture for the reader. The words used include all five senses: sight, hearing, touch, taste, and smell.

1. The birds (sang, warbled) all morning long.

2. Autos (careened, drove) around the turns at the speedway.

3. The glass animal had to be handled carefully because it was so (fragile, thin).

4. Sheila's mouth burned from the (acrid, unpleasant) sauce.

5. The overcooked vegetables were (soft, mushy).

6. The (thin, spindly) colt nuzzled his mother.

7. The (smooth, velvety) material was used for the queen's cape.

8. A radio from the next apartment (screamed, blared) into the night.

9. (Gaseous, Smelly) fumes filled the air.

10. The sweet and sour sauce had a (pleasant, tangy) taste.

11. We noticed the (agreeable, piney) odor of the Christmas tree.

12. All the machines in the shop (hummed, crackled) rhythmically.

13. The (big, massive) building was the tallest in the city.

14. A (soft, fuzzy) caterpillar crawled up my arm.

15. Our guests savored the (bland, mellow) taste of the coffee.

16. The (loud, earsplitting) siren assaulted our ears.

17. As we opened the door, we smelled a (damp, mildewy) odor coming from the very spot where we had left our wet towels.

18. The (sparkling, bright) diamond shone in the sunlight.

19. We walked noiselessly down the (quiet, hushed) hospital corridor.

20. What a (putrid, bad) smell came from the two-day-old fish!

21. The (arid, dry) earth of the desert produces only cacti.

22. The magician (charmed, entertained) everyone who watched.

23. Chris (bellowed, yelled) at the umpire behind the plate.

24. John (walked, ambled) along the street, taking his time and enjoying the beautiful day.

25. Bacon (cooked, sizzled) on the stove.

Defining the Paragraph

A paragraph is a group of sentences that work together to explain or support a central idea.

Police in Ontario are after a different kind of thief. They're chasing people who steal young trees and sell them to gardeners. The thieves' favorite tree is the blue spruce. Some gardeners pay high prices for the bluish seedlings. Thieves are taking so many that some people fear some kinds may disappear altogether.

The first sentence tells the central idea of the paragraph, that police in Ontario are looking for thieves. The rest of the sentences explain what the thieves steal and why people are worried about them. All of the sentences work together to create an organized paragraph.

Finding Sentences That Work Together. In each list of sentences, there are one or more sentences that do not work together to support a central idea. In each list, circle the letters of those sentences that *do* work together. Cross out the letters of the sentence or sentences that do not work.

Example: (a.) My friend and I made a poster on ecology.

(b.) We put pictures of endangered animals on the poster.

~~c.~~ My brother and I have a club.

1. a. People laugh when they hear about a band that plays underwater.
    b. Richard Bailey, an inventor, organized such a band in 1974.
    c. Sound waves travel more slowly underwater.
    d. Musicians dress in diving gear and play instruments they make themselves.

2. a. Deserts can be so quiet they can seem spooky.
    b. I had an uncle who went to the Sahara Desert.
    c. However, the next morning you may find dozens of tracks around your camp.
    d. You can ride across a desert all day without seeing or hearing any living creatures.

3. a. Do you know anyone who spins three ropes at one time?
    b. I do.
    c. Her name is Becky Claussen, and she puts on trick-roping shows.
    d. Maybe I would try the trampoline.

4. a. A young kangaroo, called a joey, lives in its mother's pouch.
    b. The pouch is on the front of its mother's body.
    c. Baby opossums ride on their mothers' backs.
    d. The joey moves in just after birth.

The Topic Sentence

The **topic sentence** tells what the paragraph is going to be about by stating the central idea. It is usually the first sentence in the paragraph.

The topic sentence helps you, the writer, to keep track of your ideas. If the sentences refer to the topic sentence, they will all work together.

The topic sentence also helps the reader. It states what the paragraph is going to be about.

Read the following paragraph. Notice the topic sentence in italics.

For a good old-fashioned vacation, visit lovely, historic Quebec City, Canada's oldest city. Stroll back through time down the twisting streets of Lower Town. Climb the stairs to reach Château Frontenac, an imposing castle with turrets and towers. Walk along Dufferin Terrace, the wide promenade that offers a captivating view of the St. Lawrence River. Follow the boardwalk and soon you will reach the Plains of Abraham, the scene of the battle between the French and the English that took place in 1759. Try to imagine the rolling hills crowded with fighting soldiers. How quiet it seems today! By this time you'll be ready to savor a steaming bowl of French Canadian pea soup or a delicious crêpe with maple syrup. Quebec City offers you a rare chance to breathe in the mood of yesteryear.

Identifying Topic Sentences. Read the following three paragraphs. Two of the paragraphs have a topic sentence. Underline each. One paragraph has no topic sentence. Suggest one for it, and write it on the blank.

1. You are beautiful when you smile naturally. Did you know that? Start a smile (right now!) with your eyes crinkling the wrinkles around them and bringing up the muscles of your cheeks. Isn't it a pleasant feeling? It makes others feel pleasant, too. Nobody can resist you when you smile like that.

2. You will enjoy being introduced to others if you know how to behave. Look at the person who is doing the introducing until he or she says the name of the person to whom you are being introduced. Then look at the new person's face, smile, and say, "How do you do?" Say his or her name. Give the person a good, firm handshake as you speak. If your introducer has given you a conversational clue, follow it up. With its help, you will find that you can start a conversation quite easily.

3. When Barbara gets out of bed in the morning, her first words are, "Is breakfast ready?" Orange juice, two bowls of cereal, several pieces of toast with jam, two glasses of milk—such a breakfast is standard for Barbara. At school she can hardly wait for lunch. You're likely to find her in the halls between classes eating a sandwich. And what do you suppose she says when she rushes into the house after school? "Anything in the refrigerator?"

Writing Topic Sentences 27

In writing, remember the following about the topic sentence:

1. It helps you, the writer, by keeping you on the track.
2. It makes certain that all the ideas in a paragraph relate to each other.
3. It acts as a guide by giving the reader an idea of what the paragraph is going to be about.
4. It should be clearly stated.
5. It should be interesting enough to catch the reader's attention.
6. It should let the reader know that you can cover the material adequately in the paragraph.

Writing Topic Sentences. Write a clear and interesting topic sentence for each of the following groups of sentences. Make sure that the topic sentence makes all the other sentences work together as a paragraph.

1. a. As the country becomes more crowded, the noisy activities of people drive the bald eagle away from nesting sites.

   b. Chemicals used on farms sometimes get into the eagles' food supply, and they become diseased.

   c. Habitat loss and food poisoning explain why the bald eagle is becoming an endangered species.

   d. Fewer and fewer eagles are laying eggs that hatch into normal baby birds.

TOPIC SENTENCE: _____

2. a. People first measured time by watching the changing lengths of shadows.

   b. The ancient Egyptians used the sundial to measure time.

   c. Ancient people used water clocks to tell time.

   d. The hourglass was also used by early civilizations.

TOPIC SENTENCE: _____

3. a. Her stomach was tied in knots as she watched the first contestant go through the paces.

   b. Soon, everyone would be looking at Jan to see whether she could become number one.

   c. In her mind, she rehearsed her routine.

   d. When her number flashed, she put on a smile and ran out into the crowded room.

TOPIC SENTENCE: _____

Review: Writing Paragraphs

Studying Paragraphs. In each of the groups of sentences below, underline the topic sentence of the paragraph. Cross out the letter of any sentence that does not follow the topic sentence.

1. a. The smallest dinosaurs were about the size of rabbits.

    b. The fierce, flesh-eating dinosaur, *Tyrannosaurus rex*, stood as high as a two-story house.

    c. Elephants are the biggest land-animals alive today.

    d. Dinosaurs came in a variety of sizes and shapes.

2. a. She is the most important bee in the hive.

    b. Honey has too many uses to name.

    c. Deep in every beehive lives a female bee called a queen.

    d. She lays eggs for the colony.

3. a. Their main weapon is their ability to run.

    b. Like many wild animals, cheetahs must hunt to survive and to feed their young.

    c. They can run faster than any other animal.

    d. Cheetahs are yellow with black spots.

4. a. You also need lessons.

    b. Most instructors won't teach scuba diving to anyone under twelve.

    c. To scuba dive, you need a lot of equipment.

    d. You need a suit, a mask, fins, and a tank filled with air.

Limiting the Topic Sentence. For each of the following pairs of sentences, underline the one that is limited enough to be a good topic sentence.

1. a. Many 4-H Club members raise animals.

    b. Kathryn worked hard to raise her steer.

2. a. There was jousting in Europe during the Middle Ages.

    b. In England, the most important sport in the Middle Ages was jousting.

3. a. You can do many exciting experiments at home.

    b. I have just finished an exciting experiment in our backyard.

4. a. Seven people were finalists in the contest.

    b. Gloria was one of seven finalists in the contest.

Using Sensory Details

Sensory details are most often used in developing paragraphs that describe something. These details support the statement made in the topic sentence and describe what something looks like or feels like. Jot down a list of details that you want to include in your paragraph before you start to write.

TOPIC SENTENCE:
Against the pale blue horizon was silhouetted a majestic stallion.

DETAILS:
proud head pumping up and down
muscles rippled
hooves pounded the hard earth
bounded out of sight

PARAGRAPH:
Against the pale blue horizon was silhouetted a majestic stallion. He paused at the top of a hill, his proud head pumping up and down impatiently. Each muscle in his body rippled as he turned to survey his kingdom. Then, his hooves pounded the hard earth as he bounded over the hilltop out of sight.

Developing a Paragraph Using Sensory Details. Below are two topic sentences. Use specific details to develop each into a well written paragraph. Use your imagination.

1. Out of the forest lumbered the legendary sasquatch. _____

_____

_____

_____

_____

_____

_____

2. The droning of the airplane got closer and closer. _____

_____

_____

_____

_____

_____

_____

Using Examples or Incidents

Sometimes a topic sentence may be a general idea that can best be developed through the use of several examples or an incident.

My dog really takes to water. One day I took her out on the lake in my boat. She seemed to be enjoying herself, until suddenly the boat tipped crazily, and Biscuit decided that she had had enough boating. She swam out into the lake, and all my efforts to call her back were in vain. Finally, I had to dive into the icy water myself to drag her back to the craft.

Developing a Paragraph by Using Examples. Below are topic sentences. Develop each into a well written paragraph by using several examples or an incident.

1. The first day of our vacation was nearly our last. _____

_____

_____

_____

_____

_____

2. It pays to keep trying when you're down. _____

_____

_____

_____

_____

_____

3. Some pets can certainly be mischievous. _____

_____

_____

_____

_____

_____

_____

Using Facts or Figures

Sometimes you will find it best to develop a paragraph by using facts or figures. You will move from your general topic to specific facts or statistics that support the topic. Sometimes you will want to check reference books for information to support your topic.

Whooping cranes now have something to whoop about! Thirty years ago, only twenty-one whooping cranes remained in the world. Now the number has reached ninety-nine. Many concerned people have passed laws to protect the cranes' homes in Texas, and they have also begun to raise chicks in captivity.

Developing a Paragraph by Using Facts or Figures. Develop one of the topic sentences below into a well written paragraph by using facts or figures. Be sure to indent.

1. Jobs for teenagers are scarce.
2. *Star Wars* was one of the most popular movies ever shown in our neighborhood.
3. Canadians are becoming a nation of buttonpushers.
4. It is easier to communicate today than it was a century ago.
5. Exercise is important to good health.

_____

_____

_____

_____

_____

_____

_____

_____

_____

_____

_____

_____

_____

_____

Review: Ways of Developing Paragraphs 32

Using **specific details,** write a paragraph on one of the following subjects, or choose one of your own. Begin with a strong topic sentence.

    night sounds of a city   a favorite sport

_____

_____

_____

_____

_____

_____

_____

Using **examples** or an **incident,** write a paragraph on one of the following subjects, or choose one of your own. Begin with a strong topic sentence.

    the importance of teamwork   the need for after-school sports

_____

_____

_____

_____

_____

_____

_____

Using **facts or figures,** write a paragraph on one of the following subjects, or choose one of your own. Begin with a strong topic sentence.

    the increased use of computers   strange animals of the North

_____

_____

_____

_____

_____

_____

The Narrative Paragraph (I)

The narrative paragraph is the most familiar and natural form of communication. A narrative paragraph is a paragraph that relates events.

The kind of organization most often used in the narrative paragraph is that of *time sequence*. In using time sequence, the writer tells what happened in the order that it happened.

> Kunta leaped up when the tobalo sounded at dawn. Then he, Sitafa, and their mates were running among grown-ups to the silk-cotton tree, where the village drummers were already pounding on the drums. . . . The gathering crowd of costumed villagers, one by one, soon began to respond with slow movements of their arms, legs, and bodies, then faster and faster, until almost everyone had joined the dancing.—ALEX HALEY, *Roots*

Writing a Narrative Paragraph. Write a narrative paragraph, using time sequence. Choose a topic from below or use one of your own.

Our team finally won a game last Saturday.

Terry had never been to a dance before.

Sheila learned to swim the hard way.

_____

_____

_____

_____

_____

_____

_____

_____

_____

_____

_____

_____

_____

_____

The Narrative Paragraph (II)

Narrative paragraphs will be easier if you write about things that have happened to you personally. This type of writing is called **first-person narrative** because it is you, the writer, telling about something that happened to you, rather than about something that happened to someone else.

> The ghost that got into our house on the night of November 17, 1915, raised such a hullabaloo of misunderstandings that I am sorry I didn't just let it keep on walking, and go to bed. Its advent caused my mother to throw a shoe through a window of the house next door and ended up with my grandfather shooting a patrolman. I am sorry, therefore, as I have said, that I ever paid any attention to the footsteps.—JAMES THURBER

In writing a narrative paragraph, using vivid details is particularly important in helping the reader share your experience. Details make an experience come alive.

Writing a First-Person Narrative Paragraph. Choose one of the following topic sentences, or use one of your own. Develop it into a well written paragraph, using specific details from your personal experience or your imagination.

1. Patiently, I waited on the corner for my father to come home.
2. The funniest thing happened to me last Saturday night.
3. I lost my temper, and now I regret it.

The Descriptive Paragraph (I)

A descriptive paragraph does not have much action because the writer's main purpose is to paint a picture with words. This kind of paragraph appeals to our senses, particularly those of sight and sound.

In order to make your word picture exact, you must use specific details. Instead of using general words like *walk*, *say*, and *do*, you must use more specific words like *hurry*, *shout*, and *jump*.

> The sound of Edith Jackle's voice stopped as suddenly as the voice on the radio when it is switched off. Instantly, there was quite a different sound all about them. It came from those bright things overhead, which now turned out to be birds. They were making a riotous noise, but it was much more like music—rather advanced music which you don't quite take in at the first hearing—than birds' songs ever are in our world. Yet, in spite of the singing, there was a sort of background of immense silence.—C. S. LEWIS, *The Silver Chair*

Writing a Descriptive Paragraph. Choose one of the following topic sentences, or use one of your own. Develop it into a well written descriptive paragraph, using specific details. Try to appeal to the reader's senses of sight and sound. Remember, too, the paragraph must contain only what the topic sentence says it will contain.

1. The old prospector plodded across the dusty, deserted street.
2. Everything seemed too quiet in the run-down house.
3. The cougar stalked menacingly along the ridge overlooking the cabin.

_____

_____

_____

_____

_____

_____

_____

_____

_____

_____

The Descriptive Paragraph (II)   **36**

To make ideas clear in a descriptive paragraph, *spatial order* is usually used. By spatial order, we mean the way things are situated in relation to each other in the area or space you are describing.

> When they reached the foot of the hill, they caught a glimpse of what might be rocks on each side—squarish rocks, if you looked at them carefully, but no one did. All were more concerned with the ledge right in front of them which barred their way. It was about four feet high. Then they had a stiff climb—up very rough ground for about a hundred yards, where they came to a second ledge.—C. S. LEWIS, *The Silver Chair*

Specific *direction* words, such as "each side," "right in front of them," have been used to help the reader see where all the things the writer is describing are placed in relation to each other.

Sometimes, it is not necessary to use spatial order. That is when a writer describes things in *natural order*, such as starting with a description of someone's face and moving toward that person's feet.

The topic sentence of the paragraph presents a *point of view*, the writer's way of looking at what he or she is describing. If your topic sentence is, "The spooky-looking creature was from another planet," your reader is prepared for a description of a creature not like humans. You must keep your point of view the same all through the paragraph.

The most important purpose in writing a descriptive paragraph is to create a single, unified impression in the mind of your reader.

Writing a Descriptive Paragraph. Choose a topic sentence from the following list, or use one of your own. Develop it into a descriptive paragraph, using specific details, logical space relationships, and a sustained point of view.

1. Our garage is filled with relics from the past.
2. As we entered the cave, we could hardly believe our eyes.
3. I distrusted the agent the moment I saw him.

_____

_____

_____

_____

_____

_____

_____

_____

_____

The Explanatory Paragraph (I)   37

One kind of explanatory paragraph explains *how something is done*. Instructions must be given in a logical, clear order. The best way to do this is to use the *time sequence* that you used in writing a narrative paragraph.

Developing a Logical Order. Arrange the following instructions in the order they should be placed, by numbering them in a logical order.

_____ Last, cut out the eye holes.

_____ First, slip the bag over your head.

_____ Then, with a finger rubbed in chalk, mark the eyes, nose and mouth locations on the bag.

_____ Take the bag off and decorate it in any manner you please.

____1____ You can make a creative mask out of a paper bag.

Writing an Explanatory Paragraph. Write a short paragraph, explaining how to do something. You might explain how to make a birdhouse, ride a skateboard, or do a card trick. Or you may want to use an idea of your own.

_____

_____

_____

_____

_____

_____

_____

_____

_____

_____

_____

_____

_____

_____

The Explanatory Paragraph (II) 38

Another kind of explanatory paragraph gives reasons *why* something is believed to be so. The topic sentence gives an idea or an opinion, and the other sentences in the paragraph support the opinion by giving reasons.

The usual arrangement for a "why" paragraph is to place the least important ideas first, then to move toward the most important reason or idea.

Arranging Ideas in Order. Arrange the following sentences in the order they should be placed, by numbering them in a logical order.

_____ He calls them to play with him when I am busy.

____1____ I have no life of my own with my brother Keith around.

_____ We share a room, and everytime I go to study, there he is.

_____ First, he thinks my friends are his friends.

_____ I even have to hide in the basement when I'm angry and I want to be alone!

Writing an Explanatory Paragraph. Choose one of the topic sentences below or one of your own. Write a short explanatory paragraph, using reasons to support your idea.

1. Laura is the luckiest person I know.
2. Babysitting is a good way to earn money.
3. I can hardly wait for vacation.

_____

_____

_____

_____

_____

_____

_____

_____

_____

_____

_____

_____

Review: Kinds of Paragraphs

Write a short **first-person narrative** paragraph, using a time sequence and specific details. Choose one of the following topic sentences or use one of your own.

The day was doomed from the moment I woke.
It was a dream I couldn't forget.

_____

_____

_____

_____

_____

_____

Write a **descriptive** paragraph, using specific details and a logical order. Choose one of the following topic sentences or use one of your own.

The trees looked like giants against the sky.
As we entered camp, we could smell dinner on the fire.

_____

_____

_____

_____

_____

_____

Write an **explanatory** paragraph telling *how* to do something or *why* something is so. Choose one of these topic sentences or one of your own.

Making your own kite can be easy and fun.
_____ is the best movie I've seen in a long time.

_____

_____

_____

_____

_____

_____

What Is a Composition?

A composition is *a group of related paragraphs* that work together to explain or support an idea. The first paragraph is the topic or *introductory paragraph* that tells the reader what the rest of the composition is going to be about. The next, or body, *paragraphs* work together to develop the ideas given in the introductory paragraph. The last paragraph, or conclusion, ends the composition or report by briefly summarizing the main ideas.

Identifying Parts of a Composition. Put the following paragraphs in logical, numerical order.

_____ Codes, beacon lights, and shouts are still used for communication. Although we have quicker ways of sending messages over greater distances, danger warnings are still the most urgent messages sent.

_____ Communication became important in warfare from early times. Different methods of giving orders to soldiers on the battlefield were invented. One simple system was to relay commands from one soldier to another who shouted them to the next guard. Some armies used metal shields. These acted as mirrors which reflected the sunlight. The glittering shields, when waved, could be seen over long distances. In later ages, large mirrors were used to relay signals from one receiving station to another.

_____ The most important message to be communicated was a warning of danger. Warnings by means of fire or smoke might have been the first long-distance communication signals. Many Indian tribes used smoke signals as warnings of danger. In the Revolutionary War, the colonists used beacon fires as signals.

_____ The human voice was probably the first instrument of communication. Early people no doubt groaned, grunted and shouted to each other long before they talked in words. Gestures, too, must have been used. Movements of the head, arms, and hands must have been used in passing ideas from one to another.

_____ The difficulty in using signals which can be seen or heard easily is that the enemy, too, can get the message—unless it is in code. The Romans developed a code with torches. For each letter of the alphabet a certain number of torches were placed in a certain formation. By this system it took a long time, however, to signal a message.

Finding a Subject

As a person, you are unique. There is no one else in the world just like you. Your own life, your own experiences, your own knowledge and feelings are different from those of any other person. Therefore, you have a wealth of material to write about that no one else has.

In order to write well, you don't have to experience everything personally. You must study enough to be able to write about the subject with familiarity and understanding.

Finding a Subject. Make a list of subjects of your own that might interest you. Keep your list for a future assignment.

Examples: The night my hair almost turned white
Cartoon collecting

1. _____

2. _____

3. _____

4. _____

5. _____

6. _____

7. _____

8. _____

9. _____

10. _____

11. _____

12. _____

13. _____

14. _____

15. _____

Narrowing the Subject

Once you have decided what you are going to write about, you must *narrow the subject* enough so that the material can be covered adequately in your composition or report. A topic that is too broad will either give the reader too little information or will make your composition too long.

Narrowing Subjects. Each of the following subjects is too broad to be handled in a composition. Narrow each topic so that it can be covered in a short composition.

Example: Hobbies _____*Stamp Collecting*_____

1. The Olympic Games

_____

2. Growing plants

_____

3. Our economy

_____

4. Famous men

_____

5. Famous women

_____

6. Automobiles

_____

7. Photography

_____

8. Dangerous hobbies

_____

9. Canadian heroes

_____

10. Politics

_____

Narrowing Your Subject. Now return to the list of subjects you wrote on page 41. Choose one and narrow it so that it can be covered in a short composition.

_____

Writing the Introduction

The introductory paragraph gives the reader an idea of what the composition is going to be about. It must catch the reader's attention by using carefully chosen words and interesting sentences.

Read the following introductory paragraphs:

> Once upon a time there was a little person called a hobbit. He lived in a hole. It was a comfortable hole, just right for the hobbit.

> In a hole in the ground there lived a hobbit. Not a nasty, dirty, wet hole, filled with the ends of worms and an oozy smell, yet not a dry, bare, sandy hole with nothing in it to sit down on or to eat: it was a hobbit-hole, and that means comfort.—J. R. R. TOLKIEN, *The Hobbit*

Both of these paragraphs give the reader an idea as to what the composition is going to be about, but the first paragraph is dull and uninteresting. The second paragraph catches the reader's attention. The writer has carefully chosen words to create interesting sentences.

Writing the Introduction. Using the topic that you chose for your composition, write the introductory paragraph. Make it as clear and interesting as you can. Be sure to indent.

_____

_____

_____

_____

_____

_____

_____

_____

_____

_____

_____

_____

_____

_____

Planning the Body

The *body* of the composition explains the ideas introduced in the opening paragraph. Before you write the body, you will want to arrange your ideas in a logical order. It is a good idea to make a list of the ideas. Two ways to organize ideas are *in a time sequence* or *from the least important idea to the most important one.*

Organizing Ideas. Following are two subjects with their supporting ideas. The ideas are not organized in a logical manner. Reorganize the lists by numbering the sentences properly.

1. How I became a reporter

    _____ a. We got to the studio, and I was asked to read a news story.

    _____ b. One day my mother read about auditions for *Bubblegum Digest.*

    _____ c. I dressed very carefully that morning.

    _____ d. This was a chance of a lifetime!

    _____ e. Five days later, the good news arrived!

2. A Ride on the *Maid of the Mist*

    _____ a. The closer we got to the falls, the more we got sprayed.

    _____ b. Everyone had to wear raincoats and hats.

    _____ c. What a huge amount of water came thundering over the cliffs!

    _____ d. One of the most beautiful and wettest experiences was a ride on the *Maid of the Mist* at Niagara Falls.

Planning the Body of Your Composition. You should now have your introductory paragraph written. List the ideas you wish to include in the body of your composition; then arrange those ideas in a logical order.

Introduction

1. _____

2. _____

3. _____

4. _____

5. _____

Writing the Body

After your ideas are arranged in order, your next step in writing the body is to fill in all the necessary details to explain the ideas on the list. Use specific, meaningful details. Do not add too many details, or you will confuse your reader.

Writing the Body of Your Composition. On a separate sheet of paper, write a rough draft of the body of your composition, using the ideas you listed on page 44. Be sure that all your paragraphs are related to your introduction. Then recopy the body of your composition below. Indent each new paragraph.

_____

_____

_____

_____

_____

_____

_____

_____

_____

_____

_____

_____

_____

_____

_____

_____

_____

_____

_____

_____

_____

Writing the Ending

The ending of a composition is very important. It may be a summary of what you have already written. It may be a quotation from someone else that relates to your topic; or, it may be a short, interesting statement that indicates "The End" to the reader.

The ending should be as clear, important, and interesting as the introductory paragraph. It is the last impression that your reader has of what you are telling him or her.

Writing the End of the Composition. Write an end to your composition, using one of the kinds of endings suggested: a summary, a quotation, or a short, interesting statement. Be sure to make it relate to the rest of the composition.

_____

_____

_____

_____

_____

_____

_____

_____

_____

_____

_____

_____

_____

_____

Finishing Your Composition. Now, on your own paper, rewrite your entire composition.

The Narrative Composition (I)

The narrative composition devotes attention to specific details, and tells about things in the order in which they happen. Narrative compositions can be first-person narratives in which the writer is involved in the action.

Read the following first-person narrative composition.

THE RIDE

We rarely go for leisurely rides on Saturday afternoons. It's usually too hard to get everyone assembled and harder still to get everyone to agree on an activity. This Saturday was different though, because we had just picked up our new car, and we were about to take it "for a spin" as Dad put it.

The car had that "new car" smell—a heady odor of leather, plastic, and carpet. We all piled in, anxious to see how all the various gadgets worked. We opened the windows and breathed deeply the cool, fresh scent of spring and new car.

Dad asked where we would like to go, and we all chorused, "Down by the lake!" So, off we went to cruise along the winding, hilly roads that followed the lake shore. What a smooth ride it was! The car seemed to glide over the potholes that winter had left behind. I urged Dad to go faster as we approached the ravines near the lake, but Dad declined.

Just then someone on a motorcycle passed us on the left as we rounded a bend in the road. My sister commented that we were in a no-passing zone, but I didn't see how it mattered, I retorted, since there was no other traffic on the road. Mom gave me one of those funny glances, so I changed the subject.

At the top of the next hill, another motorcyclist came up behind us and started to pass our car. At that, we noticed a big red Cadillac nosing out of a driveway up ahead. An awful moment of fear gripped us all as we watched. The cyclist saw the red car too late. Suddenly, the bike slammed into the side of the Cadillac. The impact sent the cyclist over the car and onto the pavement.

Instantly, Dad pulled over. We jumped from the car. Erin and I ran to the nearest house to call for help. Mom and Dad ran to the cyclist, and the driver of the red car joined them. To everyone's surprise, the cyclist stood up rather sheepishly. His knees were badly skinned, and there was a nasty gouge on his hand, but other than that, he was all right. Were we ever relieved!

The police and paramedics were there in a minute, and my parents made a statement for the police. The officers moved the motorcycle and cleaned up the shattered glass, all the while marveling how "that boy's helmet saved his life."

Finally, we all got back into the car. Each of us was quiet. I couldn't help but think of how I had wanted Dad to drive faster. How could I have been so dumb?

At last we pulled into our driveway with our new car. Somehow the newness of the car had worn off, but going for a ride with the family on a Saturday afternoon in spring had a whole new meaning for me.

The Narrative Composition (II)   48

The narrative composition tells "what happened." It uses the organization of *time sequence.*

Using Time Sequence in Compositions. Arrange the following topic sentences in the proper time sequence so that a composition could be written from them.

THE BIRTHDAY

_____   The table was set for the party, and balloons were popping left and right as we tried to hang them up.

_____   March 27 was my thirteenth birthday, and I had finally become a teenager.

_____   Susan James and her older brother, Steve, arrived first.

_____   Right before the party, my mother persuaded me to wear something dressier than my worn-out jeans.

_____   The kids from my class at school arrived next.

_____   During a pause in the festivities, I opened my presents.

_____   After consuming at least one ton of hot dogs, chips, hamburgers, soft drinks, and cake, we turned up the record player and started dancing.

_____   When everyone had gone, I told my parents that it was the best birthday I'd ever had.

Writing the Narrative Composition. On your own paper, write a first-person narrative composition. You may want to write about an actual experience, or you may want to use your imagination.

The Descriptive Composition (I)   49

In a descriptive composition, the writer carefully chooses details and arranges them using spatial order. That is, the writer describes things in relation to each other in an area or space.

Read the following descriptive composition about Lucy's Hobby Shop.

LUCY'S HOBBY SHOP

On Saturdays and after school hours, the quiet sidewalks of Davis Street come alive with shoppers. Those with a few extra coins in their pockets usually head for one particular store—Lucy's Hobby Shop. Sandwiched between a shoe repair shop and a health food store, Lucy's is a narrow shoe box of a store. But lack of space does not mean lack of merchandise.

The hobby shop used to be a bakery before Lucy took it over, and she kept the long glass display case that runs the length of the store. Instead of being filled with chocolate doughnuts, however, the first part of the case is loaded with balls of stringy brown rope and boxes of beads of all sizes and colors. These are the raw ingredients for macramé projects. On top of the case is a display of finished macramé projects including a purse, a belt, a wall hanging, and two plant holders. Lucy is always glad to teach her customers how to tie the knots, connect the beads, and design their own macramé creations.

The middle of the display case is a do-it-yourselfer's paradise. There are squares of tiny ceramic tiles for mosaic projects, tubes of paint in a rainbow of colors, bags of beads and stones for jewelry-making, and blocks of smooth, fragrant pine wood for carving. On top of the case sit several oil paintings, a necklace, a carved ship, and a mosaic ash tray. These are projects made by Lucy's customers, and she changes the display every few weeks.

The end of the display case near the back of the store is devoted completely to kites. Crammed into the case are instruction booklets, kits, balls of string, lengths of wood, and everything needed to build the perfect kite. Two of Lucy's own creations are hanging from the ceiling. One is an eagle-shaped kite, and the other is a red and yellow box kite. Both have been spotted flying far above the store on not-too-windy days.

What makes this hobby shop so special is Lucy herself. A short, wiry, silver-haired woman, Lucy is always working on some project, but she is never too busy to give advice and help to her customers. She can suggest the perfect hand-made birthday present for a special relative or friend, and she can usually unwind, unglue, or repatch projects that are in danger of being abandoned. She even keeps a supply of red and black licorice strings for her customers to chew on while they are mulling over their selections. It's no wonder Lucy's Hobby Shop is such a neighborhood favorite.

The Descriptive Composition (II) 50

The descriptive composition paints a word picture by appealing to the senses. It is important to choose details carefully.

The woman ran along the road.

The woman *jogged steadily* along the *gravel* road.

Notice how the second sentence provides more descriptive detail.

Choosing Details Carefully. In each of the following sentences, underline the word in parentheses that creates the better word picture.

1. Rain (fell, pattered) lightly against our window that spring day.

2. A (pungent, strong) odor filled the laboratory.

3. Our pie dough felt (tough, leathery).

4. Traffic filled the intersection and a (loud, raucous) symphony was played by the horns.

5. Our boathouse (smelled, reeked) of fish and gasoline.

6. As we walked through the forest, the ground felt (spongy, soft) under our feet.

7. Suddenly, he (crashed, came) through the closed door.

8. Sue sanded and polished the old wood until it felt (smooth, satiny).

9. Dad (winced, frowned) when he tasted my (sour, vinegary) salad dressing.

10. The (stagnant, bad) smell of standing water gave John a headache.

11. The frightened girl (spoke, stammered) during the questioning.

12. The letters (broke, crumbled) as we took them from their envelopes.

13. Immediately, a (shimmering, bright) light flooded the cavern.

14. Quickly, we all (got, scrambled) to our feet as the parade approached.

15. The (bittersweet, mellow) smell of burnt marshmallows filled the air.

Writing a Descriptive Composition. Choose a topic that you are familiar with, and write a descriptive composition. Include details that create a vivid picture for your reader. Use your own paper.

The Explanatory Composition (I)   51

The explanatory composition tells *how* something is done, or *why* something is done. The "how" composition gives directions. It is usually organized in time sequence, explaining what should be done first, what should be done next, and so on.

Study the following explanatory composition.

HOW A CLOWN MAKES UP

A clown sometimes changes his costume and often changes his act. But the one thing a clown never changes as long as he is with the circus is his facial make-up.

A clown's make-up is his trade-mark. It is his exclusive property. He may work for years to develop the character he wants to portray, and from then on that character is his alone. In the world of clowns there is an unwritten law that no clown may ever copy another clown's face.

The clown begins by covering his face completely with "clown white." This is a grease paint composed of zinc oxide mixed with glycerin and olive oil. He then puts on a stocking cap to cover up his hair. From this pure white base, he begins to create the make-believe face that all his fans know.

The clown fastens on a big, red putty nose, or one that he has made from a rubber ball. Then he paints his mouth, eyes and eyebrows with the boldest, brightest paint he can find. Over the stocking cap he puts a ragged wig. And on top of it all he places the most grotesque hat he can think of.

Because the clown's make-up is so difficult to put on and take off, he is the only performer in the circus who is allowed to eat in the cook-tent with his make-up on.

Writing the "How" Composition. On your own paper, write a composition explaining how to do something. Give the instructions in clear, logical order.

The Explanatory Composition (II) 52

The introductory paragraph of the explanatory composition includes a topic sentence that states a fact or opinion that you believe to be true. The body of the composition should explain why you believe your opinion or idea is true. Develop your composition through facts and statistics, specific examples, or incidents or anecdotes.

The explanation of "why" something is so does not always fall into a logical time sequence. You will probably find it easier to organize your ideas from the *least important to the most important* reasons why you think something is so.

Writing an Explanatory Composition. Write an explanatory composition telling "why." The following topics may give you some ideas. Use your own paper.

1. Camping is an inexpensive but enjoyable leisure activity.

2. Movies can be educational.

3. Every house should be equipped with a smoke detector.

4. We can improve the appearance of our school grounds.

5. Grocery shopping on a budget can be fun.

6. Everyone should keep up with the news.

7. Railroads are important to farmers.

8. Our cat is very fussy.

9. You can conserve energy and save money at the same time.

10. Pigs are smarter than some people may think.

Writing Friendly Letters (I)

There are five parts to a friendly letter.

1. The **heading** tells your address and the date. It is written in the upper right-hand corner and has three lines.

    Box 74
    Uxbridge, Ontario L0C 1K0
    June 18, 1982

2. The **salutation** or greeting can be casual. It is written on the line below the heading at the left margin. The first word and any other nouns are capitalized, followed by a comma.

3. In the **body** of a friendly letter, you talk to your friend. Indent the first line of every paragraph.

4. The **closing** is a simple way of saying "good-bye." This lines up with the heading. Capitalize only the first word of the closing; use a comma at the end of the closing.

5. Your **signature** is in line with the first word of the closing.

Following Correct Letter Form. Write a short letter to a friend or close relative, telling him or her about your new pet. Use the form below.

Heading _____

_____

Salutation

_____

_____   **Body**

_____

_____

_____

_____

_____

_____

_____

_____

Closing _____

Signature _____

Writing Friendly Letters (II)

In a friendly letter, you are writing to someone you know, so write as if you were speaking to that person. Write about things interesting to both of you, and answer the other person's questions or comment on his or her news at the beginning of your letter. Add plenty of details so that your letter is interesting.

Your letter should have a neat appearance. Use colorful or humorous stationery for a friend; use plain white or cream-colored stationery for an adult. Try to keep your margins straight and clear. Use black or blue ink. Most important of all, use your best penmanship.

Writing a Friendly Letter. Write a friendly letter to someone you know. Use interest, form, and appearance as your guidelines. Your friend has written to tell you that he/she likes his/her new school. Your friend has also just taken up folk dancing. In your reply, tell what activities you are in at school, and what you are doing in your spare time.

Writing Social Notes

Social notes have the same form as a friendly letter except they are much shorter. Here are the social notes you will use most frequently.

1. The **thank-you note** tells someone how much you appreciated his or her thoughtfulness. Write a note as soon as possible after receiving a gift.

2. A **bread-and-butter note** is another form of thank-you note, used after staying at someone's house. This also is to be sent as soon as possible after the event.

3. **Invitations** should include all details such as the type of activity, its purpose, where it will be held, the time and the date, and how the person should reply. R.S.V.P. means "please respond" either with a phone call, if a number is given, or with a **note of acceptance or regret.** Always answer as soon as possible.

Writing Social Notes. Write a note thanking someone for a thoughtful gift or for the wonderful weekend that you spent with that person and his or her family.

_____

_____

_____

_____

_____

_____

_____

_____

_____

_____

_____

_____

_____

_____

Writing Business Letters (I)

A business letter is a formal request for information. It is also used to order products or to complain about a product. It is brief and to the point.

The **heading** of the business letter is the same as for a friendly letter. The **inside address** is the name and address of the firm to which you are writing. It comes below the heading at the left margin. The **salutation** is formal, like *Ladies and Gentlemen, Dear Sir or Madam,* or *Dear Ms. Wills.* It is punctuated with a colon (:) and appears two lines after the inside address.

The **body** is short and states clearly the subject you are writing about. The **closing** is also formal, such as *Yours truly* or *Sincerely,* and appears on the first line below the body. Your name is typed or printed four spaces below the closing, and your **signature** is written in the space between the printed name and the closing.

Writing a Business Letter. You are writing to the Amateur Softball Association, 1483 Leacock Street, Terrace, British Columbia V8G 1B2, requesting membership, which is given free to boys and girls ages 9-17.

Heading _____

_____

Inside Address

_____

_____

_____

_____ **Salutation**

Body

_____

_____

_____

_____

_____

_____

_____

Closing _____

Signature

Printed Name _____

Writing Business Letters (II)

Choose one of the following items, and write the letter described.

1.   Open Door Enterprises produces an assortment of craft kits, each selling at $2.95. Write to the company at 15B Park West, Winnipeg, Manitoba R3R 1X1, asking them to send you either a thread design kit or a picture framing kit (you choose).

2.   If you are interested in science, write to request a copy of the Canadian Scientific catalogue. Their offices are located at 491 Maple Street, Scarborough, Ontario M1B 1Z6. Best of all, this catalogue is free.

3.   Write to the Director of the Education Department of the SPCA (Society for the Prevention of Cruelty to Animals), Box 792, Saint John, New Brunswick E1V 2K8, asking them to send you some color posters for your room. Each poster is $1.00. The titles include "Horses Need Love, Too" and "Androcles and the Lion."

Addressing the Envelope

Take the following steps when addressing your envelope:

1. Make sure that the envelope is right-side up.

2. Your return address (name, address, city, province, and postal code) goes in the upper left-hand corner.

3. The address of the receiver is centered on the envelope. Double check all numbers to make sure they are accurate. Include the correct postal code.

4. When writing to a particular department within a large company, specify the department on the envelope for faster service.

Ms. Mary Saunders
1396 St. Catherine Street W.
Montreal, Quebec
H3G 1P9

Canadian Chess Society
New Members' Department
Box 721
Prince George, British Columbia
V2L 4U3

Addressing Envelopes. Put the following address on the envelope of a business letter. Capitalize, abbreviate, and punctuate correctly. Remember to include your return address.

plays, inc. 3 bower street antigonish nova scotia B61 204

Review: Writing Letters

Writing Letters. You and your family are interested in going on a biking trip in Ontario and would like some information about where to stay. Write to: Travel Department, Ontario Youth Hostels, 43 Yonge Street, Toronto, Ontario M1S 6L3, for information on membership, facilities, and specially organized trips. You are including $1.25 to cover the cost of the pamphlet and postage. You are writing to Ms. Janet Stone.

_____

_____

_____

_____

_____

_____

_____

_____

_____

_____

_____

_____

_____

_____

_____

_____

_____

_____

_____

_____

The Classification and Arrangement of Books (I)

All the books in any library can be divided into two groups:

FICTION (stories that the author has imagined or invented)

NONFICTION (factual resources about every subject imaginable)

Fiction books are arranged alphabetically according to the author's last name. If an author has written more than one book, the books by that author are placed together on the shelf and then arranged alphabetically according to title.

Arranging Fiction Books. Number these fiction books in the order in which they should appear on the shelves.

_____ Irwin, Grace, *Least of All Saints*

_____ Price, Alfred. *Rail Life, A Book of Yarns*

_____ Sellar, Robert. *Gleaner Tales*

_____ Mowat, Farley. *The Dog Who Wouldn't Be*

_____ Hood, Hugh. *A Game of Touch*

_____ Laurence, Margaret. *The Fire-Dwellers*

Nonfiction books are usually classified according to the Dewey Decimal System. This is a system of dividing all books into ten major categories.

The Dewey Decimal System

000–099 General Works (encyclopedias, almanacs, handbooks, etc.)

100–199 Philosophy (conduct, ethics, psychology, etc.)

200–299 Religion (the Bible, mythology, theology)

300–399 Social Science (law, education, commerce, folklore, economics)

400–499 Language (languages, grammar, dictionaries)

500–599 Science (mathematics, chemistry, physics, biology, astronomy, etc.)

600–699 Applied Sciences (farming, cooking, sewing, radio, nursing, engineering)

700–799 Fine Arts (music, drawing, acting, photography, games, sports)

800–899 Literature (poetry, plays, essays)

900–999 History (biography, travel, geography)

Classifying Nonfiction Books. Where would you find these books, using the Dewey Decimal System? Write the numerical category on the blank.

1. *The World Almanac & Book of Facts* _____
2. *Workshops in Space* _____
3. *Offensive Football* _____
4. *Canada's Constitution* _____

The Classification and Arrangement of Books (II)

Every nonfiction book has its Dewey Decimal number on its spine. This number is part of the call number of the book. The **call number** is a combination of the Dewey Decimal number, the first letter of the author's name, the author's assigned number, and the first letter of the book title.

> **Book:** *The World of Champions*
> **Author:** Anthony Pritchard
>
> **Call Number:** 796.72
> P961w

Within the call number system, there are three sections that deserve special mention. These books have special codes.

1. Biography. This section includes both *biography*, a true story of a person's life written by someone else, the *autobiography*, a true story of a person's life written by that person.

920 Collective biographies (more than one person's life story). Call number 920 plus the initial of the author's or editor's last name.

> *Ten Who Dared* by Desmond Wilcox
> Call number: 920
> W

921 Individual biographies and autobiographies. Call number is 921 plus the initial of the name of the *person written about*.

> *Langston Hughes: A Biography* by Milton Meltzer
> Call number: 921
> H

2. Short Story Collections. They are marked **SC** for "Story Collection" with the initial of the author's or editor's last name placed below. They are arranged alphabetically by author's or editor's last name.

3. Reference Books. The letter **R** is placed above the classification number.

Assigning Call Number Codes. Assign call number codes to the following books. Write **920** for a collective biography, **921** for an individual biography or autobiography, **SC** for story collection, or **R** for a reference book.

1. _____ *Ten Great Mysteries*

2. _____ *Bronfman Dynasty: the Rothschilds of the New World*

3. _____ *Pope John Paul II — An Authorized Biography*

4. _____ *Guinness Book of World Records*

5. _____ *Cameras and Courage: Margaret Bourke-White*

Using the Card Catalogue (I)

The **card catalogue** contains alphabetically filed cards on each book in the library. Each card has a **call number** in the upper left-hand corner of the card.

There are usually three cards for the same book in the card catalogue: the *author card*, the *title card*, and the *subject card*. Each has the same information but is found in a different section of the file.

All types of catalogue cards give the same information:

1. The call number
2. The title, author, publisher, and date of publication
3. The number of pages and a notation on whether the book has illustrations, maps, an index, or other features.

Look at these sample cards for *Rockets and Spacecraft of the World*.

AUTHOR CARD

629.4
C   Chester, Michael

   Rockets and spacecraft of the world.
   N.Y., Norton, © 1964
      205 p., illus.

   [1] Guided missiles   [2] Rockets   [3] Satellites

      O

TITLE CARD

629.4
C   **Rockets and spacecraft of the world**

   Chester, Michael
   Rockets and spacecraft of the world.
   N.Y., Norton, © 1964
      205 p., illus.

   [1] Guided missiles   [2] Rockets   [3] Satellites

      O

SUBJECT CARD

629.4
C   **GUIDED MISSILES**

   Chester, Michael
      Rockets and spacecraft of the world.
   N.Y. Norton, © 1964
      205 p., illus.

   [1] Guided missiles   [2] Rockets   [3] Satellites
      O

1. What is the title of the book? _____

2. Who is the author? _____

3. Under what subject is this book filed? _____

Using the Card Catalogue (II)

Cross-Reference Cards. A **cross-reference card** refers you to another subject heading in the catalogue or to other subjects closely related to the one you want.

CROSS-REFERENCE
CARD

```
Rocket flight
   see
Space flight



              O
```

Guide Cards. Guide cards extend higher than other cards in the catalogue. They have letters of the alphabet, complete words, or general subject headings printed on them. They guide you to the correct place in the alphabet for the word you are looking for.

Remember, cards are filed alphabetically. *A*, *An*, and *The* do not count as first words.

Using the Card Catalogue. Number each of the following entries in the order in which you would find them in the card catalogue.

_____Taylor, Theordore

_____Outer space see exploration

_____MACRAMÉ

_____The Ukrainians helped to build Alberta

_____The Christmas ghost

_____ELEPHANTS

_____Dowdell, Dorothy

_____Electricity see energy

_____MAGIC

_____My tang's tungled and other ridiculous situations

Using Reference Materials (I)

There are many different types of reference books that provide detailed, up-to-date information.

Dictionaries. A dictionary gives the spelling, pronunciation, and meaning of a word. It also gives brief information about many subjects. **Unabridged dictionaries** are the largest and most complete. These contain well over 250 000 words with a complete history and every definition. **Abridged dictionaries** contain fewer words, but they also provide sections on biographical and geographical references. **Pocket dictionaries** should be used mainly to check spelling or to give a quick definition of an unfamiliar word.

There are **dictionaries on specific subjects,** such as art, music, or science. There are also dictionaries dealing with specific aspects of the English language. A particularly useful dictionary is a **thesaurus,** which is a dictionary of synonyms.

Encyclopedias. These books contain general articles on nearly every subject, organized alphabetically into volumes.

Using Reference Books. Which of the following reference books would you use to answer each question below? Match the question with the letter of the *most appropriate* reference.

a. *Encyclopedia of Animal Care*
b. *Roget's Thesaurus in Dictionary Form*
c. *Abbreviations Dictionary*
d. *Birds of Canada*
e. *Collier's Encyclopedia* (24 volumes)
f. *Compton's Illustrated Science Dictionary*
g. *Harvard Dictionary of Music*
h. *MacMillan Dictionary of Canadian Biography*
i. *The Mammals of America*
j. *International Dictionary of Sports and Games*

1. How did Laura Secord become a Canadian heroine?_____

2. What kind of music do madrigal singers perform? _____

3. At what age is a dog ready for obedience training?_____

4. Where does the Canada Goose like to nest? _____

5. What is CUSO? _____

6. When did Newfoundland join Canada? _____

7. What is a quarter horse?_____

8. When was hockey first played in Canada?_____

9. List six synonyms for *walk*. _____

10. What is photosynthesis?_____

Using Reference Materials (II)   65

There are several other reference books with which you should be familiar.

1. Almanacs and yearbooks are published annually. They give information on current events and historical records of government, sports, entertainment, population, and other subjects.

2. Atlases contain detailed maps of the world. They also have information about population, temperatures, and oceans.

3. Biographical reference books give detailed information about specific persons.

4. The vertical file is an alphabetical file of pamphlets, booklets, catalogucs, handbooks, and newspaper clippings about a variety of subjects, especially careers.

5. Magazines offer a larger variety of information. The *Canadian Periodical Index* lists magazine articles alphabetically by subject and author. The *Readers' Guide* is published in the United States.

Using Reference Material   On the blank, write the number of the *most appropriate* type of reference you would use to locate information on each of the following subjects.

1. The population and location of Lethbridge, Alberta _____

2. Who won the World Series last year _____

3. Pierre Trudeau _____

4. What a medical secretary does _____

5. The depth of the Indian Ocean _____

6. What is the tallest building in the world _____

7. Jacques Cousteau's childhood _____

8. How to get into college _____

9. Last month's article on Stratford in the *Canadian Theatre Review* __

10. Who is the current mayor of Kitchener _____

11. How to "adopt" an animal at your local zoo _____

12. A *Wildlife Review* article on endangered species _____

13. How many people are employed by the Canadian government _____

14. What is the per capita income in the Yukon _____

15. Who is Marie Curie and for what is she well known _____

Review: Using the Library

Using the Card Catalogue. Number these entries in the order in which you would find them in the card catalogue.

_____ DOGS

_____ Deenie

_____ Dunning, Stephen

_____ The dolphin crossing

_____ Best basketball booster

_____ Finlay, Winifred

_____ The skating rink

_____ Bongo bradley

_____ MUSIC

_____ Music in Canada

Using Reference Materials. Which reference work would be the *best* resource for information on the following? Choose from these:

dictionary, thesaurus, encyclopedia, almanac, atlas, biographical reference, vertical file, *Canadian Periodical Index*

1. map of Quebec_____

2. four synonyms for *tall* _____

3. the year the Juno Awards were first awarded _____

4. recent article on the Constitution's Charter of Rights_____

5. Louis Riel (detailed biography)_____

6. handbook of First Aid _____

7. pronunciation of *kilometre* _____

8. the function of the liver_____

Grammar, Usage, and Mechanics

The Parts of a Sentence 69

A sentence expresses a complete thought. It consists of two parts. The **subject** tells whom or what the sentence is about. The **predicate** tells what is done or what happens.

SUBJECT (who or what)	PREDICATE (what is done or what happens)
The girls	watched television.
Some people	like cold weather.
Doug Henning	performs magic tricks.

Finding the Subjects and Predicates. Draw a vertical line between the subject and the predicate in the following sentences.

Example: Everyone|laughed.

1. The Prime Minister held a news conference.

2. Each contestant chose a number from the jar.

3. The audience cheered enthusiastically.

4. Joe enjoyed his first piano lesson.

5. She listened to the news on the radio.

6. The council voted on the motion.

7. Beth and Barry cooked dinner.

8. Everyone in the world wants peace.

9. Several writers worked on the manuscript.

10. The diplomats discussed the treaty.

11. The predicate of a sentence tells something about the subject.

12. Susan locked the garage door.

13. Each skier wore a jacket and a cap.

14. Bob groped in the dark for the switch.

15. The dishwasher chugged noisily in the kitchen.

16. Lizzie's teacher agreed with the results.

17. I built these model cars.

18. Many walkers joined the hike.

19. The man with the clipboard asked some strange questions.

20. The team raised the money.

Simple Subjects and Predicates   70

In each sentence there are key words that form the basic structure of the sentence. The key word in the subject of the sentence answers the question *who?* or *what?* It is called the **simple subject.**

> The girl with the long hair|fell down.
>
> (*girl* answers *who* fell down. It is the simple subject.)

The key word in the predicate of the sentence is always the **verb.** It is called the **simple predicate.** It tells what is done or what happens.

> The girl with the long hair|fell down.
>
> (*fell* is the verb. It is the simple predicate. It tells what happened.)

Finding the Verbs and Their Simple Subjects. In each sentence, underline the verb twice and its subject once.

Example: The <u>dog</u> <u><u>barked</u></u> loudly.

1. The quick, brown fox jumped over the fence.

2. Leslie hooked a rug.

3. Seashells littered the beach.

4. Ginny entered the race.

5. Rain fell steadily all day long.

6. He remembered his old friend.

7. That roan horse gallops with a limp.

8. George heard a funny story yesterday.

9. Stars twinkled brightly in the sky.

10. The pilot landed the plane in a field.

11. The horse in that field leaped over the fence.

12. The kite lodged in the top of the tree.

13. Three beautiful packages lay under the tree.

14. Our class discussed energy conservation.

15. John's uncle explained his hobby.

Finding the Verb

A verb is a word that shows action or state of being.

Sometimes the action is one that you can see.

Warren *threw* the ball.   We *walked* home.

Sometimes the action is one that you cannot see.

Melissa *wanted* a puppy.   Tom *thought* about it.

Some verbs show that something is or exists. Such verbs tell a state of being.

The test *seemed* easy.   We *are* late.   Pat *felt* sleepy.

Finding the Verbs. Underline the verb in each of the following sentences. It may show an action you cannot see or a state of being.

1. I know a riddle.

2. It was the night before Christmas.

3. The girl rolled the clay between her hands.

4. The crowd roared its approval.

5. Karen's routine on the balance beam was excellent.

6. The rug on the floor looked dirty.

7. James dances very well.

8. Dr. Sanders performed a delicate operation.

9. The party was a success.

10. Jeffrey made the placemats.

11. Magnets attract iron and steel particles.

12. Dolores bought a pack of cards.

13. Eli Whitney invented the cotton gin.

14. We read the chapter.

15. All of the students played in the piano recital.

16. The parents enjoyed the performance.

17. The explorers discovered a lost city.

18. Dinosaurs fled from the hills.

19. The announcer was nervous before the broadcast.

20. Jennifer has an older brother.

Main Verbs and Helping Verbs

A verb may consist of a **main verb** and one or more **helping verbs,** such as *am, is, are, was, were, be, been, has, have, had, do, does,* or *did.* Sometimes the main verb will end in *-ing.*

> HV   HV   MV
> She had been watching the program.
>
>   (*Had* and *been* are helping verbs. *Watching* is the main verb.)

To find the verb in a sentence:

1. Look for a word that tells action or state of being.
2. Look for words such as *is, am, are, was, were, be, been, have, has, had, do, does, did.*
3. Look for all the words that make up the verb.

Main Verbs and Helping Verbs. Underline the verbs in the following sentences. Mark the main verb **MV** and the helping verbs **HV.**

                      HV MV
    Example: Greta has forgotten her lunch.

1. The coach was describing the next play.

2. We have watered the plants three times.

3. Roger is waiting patiently at the front door.

4. Because of the fog the plane was grounded.

5. The astronauts have arrived at the space station.

6. Five students are developing a science program.

7. He has been painting her portrait for weeks.

8. I have tasted better pies.

9. Judy is becoming a good tennis player.

10. That company has made many commercials.

11. The committee was planning the decorations for the dance.

12. I am learning French.

13. Too many bikes have been stolen.

14. Summer weather is coming earlier this year.

15. Theresa was playing her guitar softly.

Separated Parts of a Verb   73

Sometimes the parts of the verb are separated from each other by words that are not part of the verb.

The artist **has** already **finished** the painting.

Finding the Verb. In each of the following sentences, the parts of the verb are separated from each other by words that are not part of the verb. Underline the verb.

Example: We <u>had</u> not <u>seen</u> the game.

1. He had never rowed a boat before.
2. The mayor has surely heard the good news.
3. The electrician will probably fix the lights.
4. Snails have always moved slowly.
5. She did not polish her shoes.
6. Those horses had seldom run more than a mile.
7. After a few minutes, my grandmother had carefully repaired the vase.
8. Eagles are often protecting their young.
9. That taffy will quickly harden.
10. He has never beaten me in a race.

Using Verbs and Subjects. Fill in the blanks in the following sentences with a helping verb (**hv**) or a main verb (**mv**) as directed.

1. The silver car _____ easily _____ the race.
                           hv   mv

2. Snow _____ quickly _____ the town.
                 hv   mv

3. For weeks she _____ not _____ any news.
                     hv   mv

4. Janet _____ not _____ the concert.
             hv   mv

5. Bill _____ often _____ the bicycle.
           hv   mv

6. I _____ usually _____ at four o'clock.
         hv   mv

7. We _____ never _____ that program.
          hv   mv

Compound Subjects and Compound Verbs

A **compound subject** has more than one part.

> *Susan* and *Jane* saw the movie.

A **compound verb** has more than one part also.

> Terry *skipped* and *hopped*.

Identifying Compound Subjects and Compound Verbs. Underline the subjects once and the verbs twice in the following sentences.

Example: Merry swims and dives equally well.

1. Gary and Jonathan practiced a piano duet.

2. The man cooked his breakfast, washed the dishes, and ironed his shirt.

3. Terriers and poodles are both dogs.

4. The campers canoed, played games, and rode horses.

5. Marilyn's aunt and uncle are fine speakers.

6. We framed and hung the pictures.

7. Construction paper, a ruler, and scissors are needed.

8. Lisa hits and pitches well.

9. Debbie, Mitchell, and Michelle are her children.

10. Two and two make four.

11. Lions, tigers, and bears are all wild animals.

12. Gymnasts balance, tumble, and vault.

13. The kettle gurgled and sputtered on the stove.

14. The sun appeared and dried the sidewalk.

15. The ducks in the pond swam to the island and sat in the sun.

16. Cheryl and Mark have just moved here from Ottawa.

17. I answered the phone, spoke to the caller, and took a message.

18. All at once, our dog ran to the basement door and listened intently.

19. Carol and Bob ran their errands and then ate lunch.

20. The carpenters measured and cut the wood.

Subjects in Unusual Order

Placing the verb before the subject, occasionally, will make your writing more interesting. It will also give more emphasis to what you say.

USUAL ORDER: Our snoring schnauzer lay beneath the table.
UNUSUAL ORDER: Beneath the table lay our snoring schnauzer.

Finding the Subjects and Verbs. In each of the following sentences, underline the subject once and the verb twice.

1. Through the valley rode the messenger.

2. In the cockpit sat the pilot.

3. Over the river went the sleigh.

4. Among the other vegetables sprouted the onions and tomatoes.

5. Around the block skipped the children.

6. Above the horizon floated the parachute.

7. Over our heads whirled and twirled the acrobat.

8. On the other side of the table sat my brother.

9. Under the weeping willow ran the chipmunk.

10. Down the road came a silver car.

11. Beyond the trees lay safety.

12. Across the street stood the eerie old house.

13. From the kitchen came the sounds and smells of good food.

14. Quickly out of the bushes jumped the intruder.

15. Up the tree scampered the squirrel.

16. In the doorway stood a stranger.

17. Down the pipe slid the firefighters.

18. Into the store burst the angry customer.

19. On the hilltop stood the new school.

20. In the junkyard lay old tires and rusty fenders.

Kinds of Sentences

You use language for several different purposes. There is a different kind of sentence for each of these purposes.

1. A **declarative sentence** makes a statement. It tells something. A period is used after this kind of sentence.

> The sun is shining.

2. An **interrogative sentence** asks a question and ends with a question mark.

> Will you be home soon?

3. An **imperative sentence** tells or requests someone to do something. The subject is not usually stated but is understood to be "you." This sentence ends with a period.

> Please close the door.

4. An **exclamatory sentence** expresses strong feeling. An exclamation mark is used at the end.

> How surprised we were!

Classifying Sentences. Read the following sentences and decide the classification of each. Place the number that describes the sentence category in the blank.

Example: Judy is my sister. _____/_____

1. The family had a picnic on the beach. _____

2. Please set the table. _____

3. Have you seen the latest toy? _____

4. He was concerned about the outcome of the experiment. _____

5. What a happy person she is! _____

6. Cancel my order. _____

7. Everyone sang around the piano. _____

8. Please wait here. _____

9. Why do elephants have trunks? _____

10. The little girl had a bad cold. _____

11. Never speak to strangers. _____

12. How quickly this letter was delivered! _____

13. Turn off the television set now. _____

14. Who won the raffle? _____

15. What a great time we had at the toboggan party! _____

Subjects and Verbs in Questions   77

Some interrogative sentences (questions) are written in the normal order. The subject comes first, and the verb comes second.

Subject   **Verb**
Who   ordered   the pizza?

However, in other questions the subject may fall between the helping verb and the main verb.

HV   **Subject**   **MV**
Do   you   know   Ms. Fisher?

Identifying Subjects and Verbs in Questions. In each sentence below, underline the subject once and the verb twice. Remember to underline all parts of the verb.

Example: Did you find your keys?

1. Have you heard Linda Ronstadt's new song?

2. Has the morning paper come yet?

3. Is the soup done?

4. Did everyone have a good time?

5. Has Lenore cleaned her room?

6. Were you eating dinner?

7. Has money ever grown on trees?

8. Do you know a weight lifter?

9. Are Mike and Pat joining the club?

10. Have icicles formed on the windows?

11. Has the secretary gone to lunch?

12. Do you know the words to this song?

13. Have you finished your homework?

14. Did the officer blow his whistle?

15. Were the seals and penguins saved?

16. Am I getting in your way?

17. Will Sara be home soon?

18. Have you seen my notebook?

19. Does that offer still stand?

20. Were you waiting for me?

Subjects and Verbs in Commands 78

Imperative sentences (commands) usually begin with the verb. For example, in the command, *Be careful*, the verb is the first word. The subject in the sentence is *you*, even though it is not expressed. We say that the subject *you* is *understood*.

Sometimes only one word is necessary to give a command. That word is the verb. The subject is still *you* (understood).

Finding Subjects and Verbs in Commands. In each sentence below, underline the verb. Write the subject of each sentence in the blank.

1. Answer the door. _____

2. Come in. _____

3. Take the garbage out before dinner. _____

4. Hold the reins in your left hand. _____

5. Send the messenger over with the letter. _____

6. Stop. _____

7. Listen carefully to this next song. _____

8. Walk the children to the park. _____

9. Cancel my order. _____

10. Mix the cookie dough well. _____

11. After supper, call me. _____

12. Wait for the phone call from home. _____

13. Help your brother with his homework. _____

14. Be a pal. _____

15. Wind your watch. _____

16. Do your best. _____

17. Fill the gas tank. _____

18. Save one for me. _____

19. Follow the directions. _____

20. Handle that snake carefully. _____

Sentences That Begin with *There*　79

When the word *there* begins a sentence, it usually serves just to get the sentence moving. It is not the subject.

> There was nobody home. (*was* is the verb, and *nobody* is the subject.)
> Were there any fish in the lake? (*Were* is the verb, and *fish* is the subject.)

Identifying Subjects and Verbs. Underline the subject once and the verb twice in each of the following sentences.

1. There were ten rabbits in the hutch.

2. Are there any posters for sale?

3. There is a cute terrier in the window.

4. There have already been four accidents.

5. Was there any cause for worry?

6. There are two letters for you.

7. Were there any cookies on sale?

8. There was a cabin on that site.

9. On that date, there was a tremendous blizzard.

10. Was there enough electricity for the winter?

Completing a *There* Sentence. Finish each sentence below. Add the correct punctuation.

1. Will there ever be _____

2. There surely was _____

3. Has there been _____

4. There always is _____

5. Were there _____

Avoiding Sentence Fragments 80

A sentence fragment is a group of words that is not a complete thought or sentence. A sentence fragment leaves out something important, such as the subject or the verb. You may wonder *What is this about?* or *What happened?*

Threw the ball. (*Who* threw the ball?)
Kevin and his brothers. (What about them?)

Recognizing Sentences. Write **sentence** or **fragment** after each of the following.

1. After the last season _____

2. The girl threw the basketball deftly _____

3. Wondered about that _____

4. Handled the situation well _____

5. Doug gazed at the stars _____

6. Suddenly during the movie _____

7. Pick up those papers _____

8. The whole class after school _____

9. A plane landed _____

10. Deserted the sinking ship _____

Completing Fragments. Correct the following fragments by adding the words needed to make a sentence.

1. _____ followed along on his bike.

2. After the storm _____.

3. The cat and the dog _____.

4. Near our house, _____.

5. _____ after school today.

Avoiding Run-on Sentences

When two or more sentences are written incorrectly as one, the result is called a **run-on sentence.** Without a capital letter and the correct punctuation, you read right along, believing you are following one thought. Suddenly the words don't make sense, and you must back up to find where the new idea starts.

INCORRECT: The train was late we waited an hour.
CORRECT: The train was late. We waited an hour.

Correcting Run-on Sentences. Rewrite the following run-on sentences. Put in the correct capitalization and punctuation.

1. Each of us did the assignment, we finished early.

_____

2. I am leaving at five o'clock, what time is it now?

_____

3. The team members practiced their skills, they had scheduled a meet soon.

_____

4. Soap is an interesting material it's inexpensive too.

_____

5. You can "see" with your hands, try it.

_____

6. Dorothy made the arrangements, she checked with everyone.

_____

7. Alexander had a bad day, he got into trouble.

_____

8. Ann sanded the wood and cut it, she was making a birdhouse.

_____

9. Farley Mowat writes well he is my favorite author.

_____

10. Irving asked a good question, the teacher was stumped.

_____

Review: The Sentence and Its Parts 82

Underline the subject once and the verbs twice in the following sentences. Use the proper punctuation at the end of the sentence. If the subject is understood to be *you*, write it after the sentence.

1. The puppy trotted into the yard and lay down

2. Has he invented electrically heated socks for cold weather

3. I do not believe that story

4. The game went too quickly

5. Please shut the door

6. How pretty that dress is

7. Bill and Sam are giving their reports today

8. Are you a doctor

9. There were fewer students in her class this year

10. Beyond the trees lies the treasure

11. Fix and clean these roller skates

12. The chains on the swing had become rusty

Each of the following groups of words is a sentence, a fragment, or a run-on. Write **S, F,** or **R** in the blank.

1. Played basketball last night at the gym _____

2. The noise bothered us we couldn't think _____

3. Are there any other volunteers _____

4. Helped us with our work _____

5. Come over after school _____

6. Dictionaries give definitions, they are helpful to writers _____

7. Use the soap and the towels in the left drawer _____

8. The firefighters on the way to the fire _____

The Work of Verbs

The verb may tell what the subject of the sentence does. This kind of verb shows action, but the action may not be one that you can see.

The girl *jumped* over the hurdle.   The class *thought* of a solution.

The verb may show that something exists. It may tell about a state of being.

Debby *seems* happy.   The dog *is* thirsty.

Verbs show action or state of being.

Identifying the Verbs. Underline the verb in each sentence.

Example: We <u>walked</u> to the corner.

1. Jeff seemed tired after the game.

2. School closed for the year.

3. Sandy tipped the basketball away from the center.

4. Old dogs learn new tricks.

5. The name of the show was *Annie*.

6. Dr. Jekyll became Mr. Hyde.

7. The bird floated lazily in the blue sky.

8. That salesperson is my mother.

9. Gary watches television all the time.

10. All the parents applauded the children's efforts.

Using Verbs. Add a verb to each sentence below.

1. The skater _____ on the ice.

2. Planes _____ over the house.

3. The drummer _____ serious.

4. Out of the hat _____ the magician's rabbit.

5. This _____ the end.

Verbs and Direct Objects

The **direct object** tells who or what receives the action of the verb.

To find the direct object in a sentence, first find the verb. Then ask *what?* or *whom?* after the verb.

The dog chewed my *slippers*.   (chewed *what? slippers*.)
I saw *Ernie* at the store.   (saw *whom? Ernie*.)

Using Direct Objects. Add direct objects to the following sentences.

1. The boys read the _____.

2. May I ride my _____ after school?

3. The big dog chased the _____.

4. Louis threw _____ at the tin cans.

5. Susan built a _____ for her books.

6. Everyone followed _____.

7. Charles Lindbergh flew the _____ over the Atlantic Ocean.

8. Please bring your _____ to school today.

9. Bruce Cockburn recorded a new_____.

10. French troops surrounded _____.

Identifying Verbs and Direct Objects. Underline the verb and circle the direct object.

Example: The orchestra <u>played</u> the music

1. Tony made the dinner.

2. Debby practiced the piano every day.

3. Robin caught a large fish.

4. The gymnast started her exercises.

5. The gardener fertilized the flowers.

6. Scientists find answers to many problems.

7. The spider carefully spun its web.

8. Pour the wax into the mold.

9. Morgan smacked the ball out of the park.

10. Underline the verb.

Transitive and Intransitive Verbs 85

When there is a word in a sentence that answers the question *whom?* or *what?* after the verb, that word is a *direct object*. Verbs that have direct objects are called **transitive verbs.**

  Joan *moved* the lamp. (transitive verb)

When a verb does not have a direct object, it is called an **intransitive verb.**

  Joan *moved* to Windsor. (intransitive verb)

Identifying Transitive and Intransitive Verbs. In the following sentences, underline each verb. Then write **T** if the verb is transitive or **I** if the verb is intransitive.

  Example: The door <u>flew</u> open. ____*I*____

1. The ninth graders carried their notebooks. _____

2. Divide the cards into four piles. _____

3. The monkeys peeked through the bars of their cages. _____

4. The boys laughed during the movie. _____

5. The dictionary lay on the table. _____

6. Pete set the table for dinner. _____

7. The dentist examined my teeth. _____

8. The telephone rang several times. _____

9. John spoke quickly. _____

10. Louise and Rhoda made several clever posters. _____

11. The captain sailed the ship past the rocks. _____

12. Their quarterback moved too quickly for us. _____

13. Everyone drank the lemonade slowly. _____

14. I smelled the overripe bananas. _____

15. Jill sees well with her new glasses. _____

16. The Russian bought an American car. _____

17. The merchant felt the woolen cloth. _____

18. The dancer walked slowly toward the entrance. _____

19. He heard better with his new hearing aid. _____

20. The children hid in the closet during the game. _____

Linking Verbs

Verbs that show a state of being are called **linking verbs.** Some linking verbs are *is, am, are, was, were, be, become, seem, look, appear, smell, taste,* and *sound.* Linking verbs do not have a direct object. They connect the subject with a word in the predicate.

LINKING VERB: The boy *is* an artist. (*artist* is linked to *boy.*)
Joyce *appeared* unconcerned. (*unconcerned* describes *Joyce.*)

TRANSITIVE VERB: The boy *drank* the milk. (milk is the *direct object.*)

Identifying Linking Verbs. Underline the subject once, and the linking verb twice. Then draw a circle around the word linked to the subject.

Example: The woman is a poet.

1. Dale became president of the class.
2. The newly fallen snow looked clean.
3. Henry felt tired after the marathon.
4. Smoking is hazardous to everyone's health.
5. Did Judy seem unhappy?
6. The band sounded good at the football game.
7. Mr. Pritchard is the new teacher.
8. Kris appeared older in her new dress.
9. The members of the track team were eager for the meet.
10. Those small dogs are loud.

Identifying Linking Verbs and Transitive Verbs. In each sentence, underline the verb. On the blank, write **L** if the verb is linking, or **T** if the verb is transitive.

1. The ice cream soda was good. _____

2. The sergeant pulled the alarm. _____

3. Gymnastics is my favorite sport. _____

4. She sanded the rough edge of the wood. _____

5. The boxer appeared groggy. _____

6. Mary sounded excited about her new record. _____

7. Were you late for class? _____

8. Be careful. _____

9. John liked the chocolate cupcakes. _____

10. The cupcakes tasted delicious. _____

Parts of the Verb

A verb often consists of more than one word. Each main verb may have one or two helping verbs with it, such as *is, do, has, have*. Here are some additional helping verbs.

will go	**can** go	**would** go	**could** go	**must** go
shall go	**may** go	**should** go	**might** go	

The words that make up a verb are sometimes separated by other words that are not verbs.

should not *have gone*   *will* probably *arrive*
might never *have happened*   *could* barely *understand*

Identifying Parts of the Verb. Write **hv** over the helping verbs and **mv** over the main verbs in the following sentences.

Example: Brett might have gone to the movies.

1. The scouts will have a float in the parade.

2. Jane could never finish a whole pizza.

3. She may have gone to the store at the corner.

4. Did you go to the Ice Capades this year?

5. You should have closed the door.

6. The next batter will probably hit the ball out of the park.

7. Pam should remember the message.

8. I will wait for you.

9. The girl might have talked to the teacher.

10. Can you play backgammon?

Using Helping Verbs. The following sentences have main verbs but no helping verbs. Write the helping verbs in the blanks provided.

1. We _____ never seen such a sight.

2. You _____ always cross the street at the corner.

3. They _____ _____ read that book before.

4. _____ you throw the ball hard?

5. _____ you made your costume yet?

Tenses of Verbs

Verbs change their forms to show the time that they tell about. These changes in form to show the time are called **tenses.**

Tense changes are made in these three ways:

1. By change in spelling: ring, rang, rung
2. By change in ending: talk, talked
3. By changes in helping verbs: has talked, will talk

Here are five important tenses:

PRESENT TENSE	She calls	We speak
FUTURE TENSE	She will call	We shall speak
PAST TENSE	She called	We spoke
PRESENT PERFECT TENSE	She has called	We have spoken
PAST PERFECT TENSE	She had called	We had spoken

Identifying Tenses. Underline the verb in each sentence. Identify the tense in the blank at the right.

1. She wakes early every morning. _____

2. Have you found your bracelet yet? _____

3. The dog chased the cat. _____

4. Answer the phone. _____

5. Debby will light the candles tonight. _____

6. The choir practiced all week. _____

7. Are you ready for the test? _____

8. We had finished our homework early. _____

9. Was your mother angry? _____

10. My brother and I will go to the movies tomorrow. _____

Using Tenses. Write the correct form of the verb for each sentence.

Example: Brad (present perfect of go) to work. *has gone*

1. Harvey (past of *read*) a mystery book. _____

2. The girl (future of *graduate*) in June. _____

3. Barb (present perfect of *learn*) the trick easily. _____

4. Greg (past perfect of *see*) Star Wars four times. _____

5. The home team (present of *win*) consistently. _____

The Principal Parts of Verbs (I)   89

The principal parts of a verb are the present tense, the past tense, and the past participle. If you know the principal parts of a verb, you can make any tense by using the forms alone or with helping verbs.

There are several thousand verbs in the English language. Most of them cause no problems of usage at all. They are **regular verbs.** That is, the past tense is formed by adding *-ed* or *-d* to the present. The past participle is the same as the past tense form and is always used with a helping verb.

PRESENT	PAST	PAST PARTICIPLE
study	studied	(have) studied
like	liked	(have) liked

Identifying the Principal Parts of Regular Verbs. Write the principal parts of the following regular verbs.

	PRESENT	PAST	PAST PARTICIPLE
1. jump	_____	_____	_____
2. push	_____	_____	_____
3. love	_____	_____	_____
4. move	_____	_____	_____
5. shape	_____	_____	_____
6. skate	_____	_____	_____
7. fix	_____	_____	_____
8. watch	_____	_____	_____
9. erase	_____	_____	_____
10. kick	_____	_____	_____
11. carry	_____	_____	_____
12. like	_____	_____	_____
13. finish	_____	_____	_____
14. wash	_____	_____	_____
15. type	_____	_____	_____

The Principal Parts of Verbs (II)   90

There are a few commonly used verbs whose past forms do not follow a regular pattern. They are **irregular verbs.**

When using irregular verbs, remember two important things:

1. The past tense is always used by itself, *without* a helping verb.

2. The past participle is always used *with* a helping verb.

Identifying Principal Parts of Irregular Verbs. Write the principal parts of the following irregular verbs.

	PRESENT	PAST	PAST PARTICIPLE
1. break	break		
2. bring		brought	
3. choose			
4. come			
5. do		did	
6. drink			(have) drunk
7. eat			
8. freeze	freeze		
9. give			
10. go			
11. grow		grew	
12. know			
13. ride			
14. ring			
15. run	run		
16. see			
17. sing			
18. sit		sat	
19. speak			(have) spoken
20. steal		stole	
21. swim			
22. take			
23. throw	throw		
24. wear			(have) worn
25. write			

Practice with Irregular Verbs (I) 91

Underline the correct word from the two given in parentheses.

1. The waiter (bring, brought) the food.

2. Have you ever (bring, brought) your mother flowers?

3. John (bring, brought) back his library books.

4. The lawyer will (bring, brought) the documents to us.

5. Didn't she (bring, brought) her tennis racket?

6. Many have (bring, brought) their own horses.

7. (Bring, Brought) that here!

8. Darlene's mother (bring, brought) her a present.

9. We accidentally (broke, broken) the new mobile.

10. That chair has been (broke, broken) for a long time.

11. Wasn't his watch (broke, broken) yesterday?

12. The cheerleader might have (broke, broken) her leg.

13. The promise was (broke, broken).

14. Sam (broke, broken) the egg into the bowl.

15. The record has been (broke, broken).

16. Your bike will be (broke, broken) if you're not careful.

17. The clerk (comes, come) in at noon.

18. The moon (came, come) over the mountain.

19. The moment has (came, come) to tell the truth.

20. They have (came, come) in late every day.

21. The dog had (came, come) when he was called.

22. You should have (came, come) to the party.

23. When will your sister (came, come) home from college?

24. Several packages have (came, come) to the house.

25. The report cards have (came, come) in the mail.

Practice with Irregular Verbs (II)

Underline the correct word from the two words given.

1. Shawn was (chose, chosen) class president.

2. Which book have you (chose, chosen)?

3. The girl (chose, chosen) an interesting topic for her report.

4. I would have (chose, chosen) yogurt for dessert.

5. Last summer Adam (chose, chosen) to go swimming every day.

6. People (chose, chosen) their own partners.

7. The last contestant in the show was (chose, chosen) for the role.

8. Will the winner be (chose, chosen) today?

9. Betty (did, done) her best.

10. Who (did, done) it?

11. What damage has been (did, done)?

12. The dishes will be (did, done) immediately after dinner.

13. The dogs (did, done) the same trick over and over.

14. Mr. Jones might have (did, done) that picture.

15. My homeroom (did, done) that collage.

16. What would you have (did, done)?

17. I (did, done) the work myself.

18. Bob (drank, drunk) his cola too quickly.

19. How much orange juice have you (drank, drunk)?

20. The animals (drank, drunk) from the stream.

21. Four glasses of lemonade had been (drank, drunk).

22. I never (drank, drunk) plum juice before.

23. The soda had been (drank, drunk) before the food was eaten.

24. Jason (drank, drunk) all his medicine.

25. Linda and Jenny had never (drank, drunk) carrot juice.

Practice with Irregular Verbs (III)   93

Underline the correct word from the two words given.

1. Have you (ate, eaten) in a restaurant lately?

2. The big fish (ate, eaten) the little fish.

3. I have (ate, eaten) too much candy today.

4. The slices of pizza have all been (ate, eaten).

5. The workers (ate, eaten) late.

6. Maureen and Monty had (ate, eaten) at their aunt's house.

7. Which dog food was (ate, eaten)?

8. Half of the apple had been (ate, eaten).

9. Her smile (froze, frozen) on her face.

10. The mammoth was (froze, frozen) in the ice.

11. Ice cubes (froze, frozen) in the tray.

12. Weren't your hands (froze, frozen) without mittens?

13. The cook had (froze, frozen) the leftovers.

14. We nearly (froze, frozen) while waiting in line.

15. The water had been (froze, frozen) into many shapes.

16. It was so cold that the pond was (froze, frozen) solid.

17. Steven (gave, given) his grandmother a watch.

18. Have you (gave, given) Lauren her present?

19. The verdict had been (gave, given).

20. Money was (gave, given) to charity.

21. The doctor (gave, given) the woman a flu shot.

22. That answer has been (gave, given) before.

23. Grades will be (gave, given) tomorrow.

24. I should have (gave, given) the waitress a larger tip.

25. The coach (gave, given) the rookie a starting assignment.

Practice with Irregular Verbs (IV)

Underline the correct word from the two words given.

1. The thieves (went, gone) down that alley!

2. Have you (went, gone) to the movies lately?

3. We should have (went, gone) to the meeting.

4. The cab driver (went, gone) around the block.

5. Justin and Chris (went, gone) skating.

6. The detective had (went, gone) to Regina.

7. I have never (went, gone) to Calgary.

8. Our family (went, gone) on a vacation.

9. The girls (grew, grown) their own food at camp.

10. How many centimetres has Ed (grew, grown) since last year?

11. We have (grew, grown) tomatoes this year.

12. Most of the zucchini had (grew, grown) too large.

13. For her biology project, Liz (grew, grown) two groups of beans.

14. His fame should have (grew, grown).

15. My father (grew, grown) a beard this year.

16. The air has (grew, grown) cold.

17. Few (knew, known) the true facts of the case.

18. Had you (knew, known) that teacher before?

19. The mail carrier should have (knew, known) your address.

20. You should have (knew, known) the answer.

21. The visitor (knew, known) our neighbors very well.

22. How long have you (knew, known) about this?

23. Princess Anne has (knew, known) the art of horsemanship since she was very young.

24. I hadn't (knew, known) about the test.

25. She has (knew, known) the Lewis family for five years.

Practice with Irregular Verbs (V)

Underline the correct word from the two words given.

1. He (ran, run) for his life.

2. Have you (ran, run) all your errands today?

3. This train has (ran, run) to Toronto for years.

4. Prices of hats have (ran, run) as high as fifty dollars.

5. The marathon was (ran, run) yesterday.

6. Mr. Williams (ran, run) his business efficiently.

7. Enemy ships had (ran, run) the blockade.

8. We should have (ran, run) two kilometres today.

9. The bells (rang, rung) joyously throughout the village.

10. The doorbell had (rang, rung) four times.

11. The room (rang, rung) with shouts of laughter.

12. Have you ever (rang, rung) the bell at the carnival?

13. The church bells were (rang, rung) on Sunday.

14. I could have (rang, rung) the doorbell, but I knocked instead.

15. The chimes in the tower have (rang, rung).

16. We had (rode, ridden) along to keep my uncle company.

17. The commuter (rode, ridden) the train every morning.

18. Has Judy ever (rode, ridden) on the roller coaster?

19. The ship (rode, ridden) the waves.

20. Ms. Evans and Ms. Porter (rode, ridden) their bikes to school.

21. I have (rode, ridden) the train two times.

22. Our family (rode, ridden) into town together.

23. Susan had (rode, ridden) in a horse show.

24. The farmer had not (rode, ridden) the new tractor yet.

25. Who (rode, ridden) the snowmobile last?

Practice with Irregular Verbs (VI)

Underline the correct word from the two words given.

1. The bluebird (sang, sung) sweetly on the branch.

2. Has James ever (sang, sung) professionally?

3. John and Sylvia will have (sang, sung) six times by Friday.

4. When I (sang, sung) by myself in music class, I was nervous.

5. The family (sang, sung) together around the old piano.

6. How well the choral group (sang, sung)!

7. The soprano should have (sang, sung) a solo.

8. I (sang, sung) off-key because of my cold.

9. I thought I (saw, seen) my brother leave.

10. Have you (saw, seen) the new movie?

11. The boy should have (saw, seen) the car.

12. The spectators (saw, seen) a great tennis match.

13. That was the best basketball game I've ever (saw, seen).

14. Where was the car last (saw, seen)?

15. I (saw, seen) to it that the work was done well.

16. Ms. Sawyer had never (saw, seen) such good work.

17. Have you (spoke, spoken) to your mom about this?

18. Has Joy ever (spoke, spoken) French?

19. "I've (spoke, spoken) to you three times," complained Mr. Vogel.

20. Dick and Davis (spoke, spoken) to their friends about the project.

21. The hermit had not (spoke, spoken) to anyone for months.

22. The scientist (spoke, spoken) on television last night.

23. The police officer should have (spoke, spoken) to the children.

24. The lawyer for the accused (spoke, spoken) to the jury.

25. My father has (spoke, spoken) of you often.

Practice with Irregular Verbs (VII) 97

Underline the correct word from the two words given.

1. Fish (swam, swum) in schools through the water.

2. He (swam, swum) his horse across the pond.

3. Have you ever (swam, swum) in a creek?

4. The relay team had (swam, swum) four lengths of the pool.

5. The shark (swam, swum) around the boat.

6. I will have (swam, swum) two kilometres when I reach the raft.

7. The catcher (threw, thrown) to first base.

8. They had (threw, thrown) the Count of Monte Cristo in jail.

9. Have you (threw, thrown) away your old sweatshirt?

10. The engineer (threw, thrown) the switch.

11. The passengers were (threw, thrown) to the ground by the crash.

12. The pitcher had (threw, thrown) a perfect game.

13. She (wore, worn) a beautiful white dress.

14. Who would have (wore, worn) glass slippers?

15. Have those socks been (wore, worn) lately?

16. These gloves are (wore, worn) out!

17. It became colder as the day (wore, worn) on.

18. The Novocain had (wore, worn) off, and my mouth felt better.

19. The check had been (wrote, written) two days ago.

20. Honesty was (wrote, written) all over his face.

21. The girl (wrote, written) her pen pal a letter.

22. Daniel Hill has (wrote, written) a book called *The Freedom-Seekers*.

23. Have you ever (wrote, written) a poem?

24. The teacher (wrote, written) the assignment on the board.

25. We have (wrote, written) a play for our family.

Choosing the Right Verb: *Let* and *Leave*

Let means "permit."

> *Let* me go.

Leave means "go away (from)." *Leave* also means "allow to remain."

> *Leave* the room. (go away from)
> They will *leave* the books on the table. (allow to remain)

The principal parts of these verbs are:

> **let, let, let   leave, left, left**

Choosing the Right Verb. Underline the correct word from the two words given.

1. (Let, Leave) those packages alone.

2. Will your mother (let, leave) me stay for dinner?

3. Did you (let, leave) your key in the car?

4. The student (let, left) his homework slide.

5. They had never (let, left) us do that before.

6. Please (let, leave) the cookies cool before you eat them.

7. Please (let, leave) the window open.

8. Jan and Phil will (let, leave) us a note.

9. My father (let, leave) me go to work with him.

10. When can you (let, leave) for Florida?

11. "Sesame Street" will (let, leave) the air for the summer.

12. They (let, left) the visitor into the house.

13. (Let, Leave) the boy stay in the ballpark.

14. May I (let, leave) the table?

15. He will (let, leave) his job in two weeks.

16. (Let, Leave) me stay until five o'clock.

17. She may (let, leave) her hair grow.

18. The water skier forgot to (let, leave) go of the tow rope.

19. The crew will (let, leave) us come aboard the ship.

20. Marie Antoinette supposedly said, "(Let, Leave) them eat cake."

Choosing the Right Verb: *Lie* and *Lay*

Lie means "recline" or "rest." It has no object. Its principal parts are **lie, lay, lain.**
Lay means "put" or "place." It takes an object. Its principal parts are **lay, laid, laid.**

Choosing the Right Verb. Underline the correct word from the two words given.

1. After he dries them, Ron (lies, lays) the dishes on the table.

2. Sandy (lay, laid) down for a rest.

3. The dog will (lie, lay) down on the grass.

4. (Lie, Lay) the baby down gently.

5. The bricklayer (lay, laid) five hundred bricks in a short time.

6. Twelve eggs were (lain, laid) by one hen.

7. The patient was (lying, laying) down on the couch.

8. (Lie, Lay) down when you get too tired.

9. How long has the cat (lain, laid) there?

10. Suddenly the runner (lay, laid) down in the middle of the track.

11. (Lie, Lay) the presents on the floor.

12. Joyce (lay, laid) the books on the shelf.

13. The turtle will (lie, lay) on that rock all day.

14. Sally and her sister were (lying, laying) on the beach.

15. The ship will (lie, lay) to the south of us.

16. Toys (lay, laid) all over after the birthday party.

17. My father (lay, laid) his keys down.

18. The treasure (lies, lays) hidden in the ocean.

19. The reporter (lay, laid) her briefcase on the chair.

20. The workers will (lie, lay) the new carpet in the hall.

Choosing the Right Verb: *Sit* and *Set*

Sit means "rest" or "be seated." *Sit* does not take an object.

Sat is the past tense of *sit*. It means "rested" or "was seated." Since *sat* is a form of *sit*, it does not take an object.

Set is a different word entirely. It means "put" or "place." *Set* takes an object.

The principal parts of these verbs are:

sit, sat, sat   set, set, set

Choosing the Right Verb. Underline the correct word from the two words given.

1. The guests will (sit, set) in the front row.

2. (Sit, Set) the mail on the table.

3. Who will (sit, set) in the front row?

4. The clock has (sat, set) on that ledge for a long time.

5. We had to (sit, set) in the end zone.

6. Adam has (sat, set) quietly for a long time.

7. Carol (sit, set) the lamp near the couch.

8. (Sit, Set) the dishes on the table.

9. Mrs. Young will (sit, set) on the Council if she wins.

10. Have you (sit, set) the mousetrap out yet?

11. Everyone on the bus (sat, set) down.

12. (Sit, Set) your report card on the counter.

13. Will you (sit, set) your books on the desk?

14. The students may (sit, set) in the library and read.

15. When will we be able to (sit, set) down?

16. I had to carry the box because there was no place to (sit, set) it down.

17. How long will we (sit, set) in the doctor's office?

18. Our dog can (sit, set) and watch the squirrels for hours.

19. Peter had (sit, set) the pencils on the table.

20. Please (sit, set) with us on the porch for a while.

Review: Using Verbs

Identifying Transitive and Intransitive Verbs. Find the verb in each of the following sentences. If the verb is *transitive*, underline it and circle the direct object. If the verb is *intransitive*, underline only the verb.

Example: The girl bought a scarf.   The girl was pretty.

1. John hit the ball out of the park.

2. Sunflowers grow very tall.

3. Gail wanted her own horse.

4. The dolphins played happily in the water.

5. Were you prepared for the quiz?

Identifying the Tenses. Underline the verb in each sentence. Then name the tense in the blank. The five tenses used are the *present, future, past, present perfect,* and *past perfect.*

1. Have you written to your cousins lately? _____

2. The dog sits quietly by the window. _____

3. I threw the garbage out. _____

4. When will you deliver the message? _____

5. We had eaten the entire pizza. _____

Using Verbs Correctly. Underline the correct verb from the two words given in parentheses.

1. Have you (bring, brought) your material for sewing?

2. Someone has (drank, drunk) all the milk.

3. Howard (give, gave) me a book about Bigfoot.

4. Clare had never (went, gone) tobogganing before.

5. I (ran, run) six kilometres yesterday.

6. On his way home, Chuck (saw, seen) the accident.

7. He had never (saw, seen) so many cars in one spot.

8. Beth has (write, written) a letter to the editor.

9. You should have (came, come) to the meeting.

10. She had (grew, grown) taller during the summer.

What Are Nouns?

A noun is a word used to name a person, place, or thing.
Things named by nouns may be things you can see:

    chair   tree   Lake Louise   light   Canada

Other things named by nouns may be things you cannot see:

    history   song   speech   patience   rules

Still other things named by nouns are ideas:

    friendship   fairness   honesty   happiness   love

Identifying Nouns. Underline the nouns in each of the following sentences. There is more than one noun in each sentence.

1. Snow covered the mountain.

2. The water flowed gently down the hillside.

3. Honesty is the best policy.

4. There was an old car in the garage.

5. Lightning told the boy that the storm was coming.

6. Gordon Pinsent narrates the program.

7. Horses, cows, and chickens live on that farm.

8. My favorite subjects in school are science and math.

9. The gymnasium was filled with anxious spectators.

10. The family had a reunion.

11. Summer is the warmest season of the year.

12. The green leaves turned golden in the autumn.

13. Suddenly, a monster appeared in the darkness.

14. The trees danced in the wind.

15. Ponies are little horses.

16. Grasshoppers have strong muscles in their legs.

17. The house was covered with ivy.

18. The lifeguard saved the lives of two children.

19. The swan swam closer to our boat.

20. The class studied the history of Spain last semester.

Common Nouns and Proper Nouns 103

A common noun is the name of a whole class of persons, places, or things. It is a general name and does not refer to a special person, place, or thing.

A proper noun is the name of a particular person, place, or thing. It always begins with a capital letter. It may also consist of more than one word.

COMMON NOUNS	PROPER NOUNS
girl	Julie Anderson
road	Sandy Hook Road
store	Super-Value Food Store

Finding the Proper Nouns. Supply capital letters where needed in the following sentences.

Example: jane went to chilliwack.

1. Our house is on the corner of rupert avenue and dempster street.

2. The watsons traveled to regina, saskatchewan, and red deer, alberta.

3. Next thursday is my birthday.

4. susan and rita live on grove street.

5. william shakespeare wrote many plays.

Determining Proper Nouns. For each common noun that is given, write a proper noun in the blank.

1. month _____

2. day _____

3. dog _____

4. city _____

5. movie _____

6. store _____

7. cereal _____

8. holiday _____

9. toy _____

10. vehicle _____

Nouns Used as Subjects

The subject of a sentence tells who or what is being talked about. Nouns are often used as subjects.

    S   **V**
Jane entered the room quietly.

      S   **V**
Thousands filled the stadium.

Sometimes the subject is not right next to the verb. Other words may separate them.

    S   **V**
Jane always entered the room quietly.

     S   **V**
Thousands of people filled the stadium.

Finding the Nouns as Subjects. Underline each of the nouns used as subjects in the following sentences.

1. Kenny Rogers is my favorite singer.

2. Part of the paper was torn.

3. The pen with the felt tip wrote well.

4. Cinnamon is a spice.

5. Into the pond waddled a duck.

6. Out of the tree flew a colorful bird.

7. There were several players chosen for the racquetball game.

8. Nancy Drew followed the clues on the map.

9. That woman became the superintendent.

10. The scrimmage lasted one hour.

11. There was only one solution to the puzzle.

12. Six cats ran across the street.

13. The members of the team were satisfied.

14. Many people eat fattening foods.

15. The bicycle in the garage has a flat tire.

Nouns Used as Direct Objects

A noun used as a direct object receives the action of a transitive verb.

Gary threw the *ball*. (What did Gary throw? The *ball*.)
Angie saw the *dentist*. (Whom did Angie see? The *dentist*.)
We have a *surprise* for you. (What do we have? A *surprise*.)

Identifying Direct Objects. Underline the noun used as a direct object in each of the following sentences.

1. The rocket is circling the earth.

2. Ms. Treadwell needed a new car.

3. My father's dog chases the neighbor's cat.

4. Questions usually have answers.

5. St. George slew the ferocious dragon.

6. Did you understand the assignment?

7. Follow the leader.

8. Some elephants have enormous tusks.

9. The baker with the white chef's cap baked sourdough bread.

10. That sentence has a mistake in it.

11. The octopus waved its tentacle at a friend.

12. My cousins and I ate a whole pie.

13. The boy delivered a long telegram.

14. The creatures landed their spaceship on our property.

15. Who baked the pie?

16. The child nearly lost her way in the dark.

17. A king ruled the early Sumerian cities.

18. You can read this story for us.

19. Each word has three syllables.

20. Who leads the National League in home runs?

Nouns Used as Indirect Objects 106

The indirect object tells to whom (or to what) or for whom (or for what) the action of the verb applies.

Jennifer gave *Robert* the book. (*Robert* is the indirect object.)

A sentence contains an indirect object only if there is also a direct object. The indirect object lies between the verb and the direct object. The words *to* and *for* never appear before the indirect object.

Finding Indirect Objects. Underline the noun used as an indirect object in each of the following sentences.

1. Debby showed Paula the latest dance step.

2. The school mailed the new students their registration forms.

3. Some horses give trainers many problems.

4. We should have told Sylvia the truth.

5. Mr. Stevens gave his car a tune-up.

6. The pitcher threw the batter a curve.

7. The vendor gave each child a balloon.

8. Has Mary given Olivia the letter?

9. He gives the little kids a hard time.

10. The teacher assigned Sheila the problem.

11. My mother bought our family a new game of Scrabble.

12. France gave Spain the territory.

13. Has the merchant sold Pat the bike?

14. The coach told the team the rules.

15. Can you give the class any helpful suggestions?

16. The principal found my brother a job.

17. Will you show the artist your painting?

18. Give your friend his calculator.

19. Brenda loaned Larry her new record.

20. Ms. Perkins showed the students the costumes for the play.

Predicate Nouns

A noun in the predicate of the sentence linked to the subject by a linking verb is called a **predicate noun.** It usually means the same thing as the subject. In many sentences the predicate noun and the subject can be exchanged without changing the meaning.

> The dog is a *poodle.* (*poodle* is a predicate noun.)
>
> The *poodle* is a dog. (Now *poodle* is the subject.)

Identifying Predicate Nouns. Underline the predicate noun in each of the following sentences.

1. My sister is a good pitcher.
2. Edward Asner became the star of that television program.
3. Peaches are my favorite summer fruit.
4. That automobile was a classic.
5. Vegetables are nourishing foods.
6. The pink-eyed, white cat is an albino.
7. The C.N. Tower is the tallest structure in the world.
8. Those horses were stallions.
9. Brett has become a good mechanic.
10. Craig and Mark are twins.

Choosing Predicate Nouns. In the blank, tell whether the word in italics is a **predicate noun** or a **direct object.**

Example: The man was a *detective.* ___*predicate noun*___

The man hired a *detective.* ___*direct object*___

1. Julia canceled her *party.* _____
2. The "meeting" was really a surprise *party.* _____
3. The girl entered the *classroom.* _____
4. The outdoors became our *classroom* for a day. _____
5. Ronnie is my best *friend.* _____
6. Ronnie will always help a *friend.* _____
7. Sally is the *star* of the school play. _____
8. I saw a *star* in the winter sky. _____
9. Dean Martin and Jerry Lewis were a *team.* _____
10. Bud Grant chose this year's *team.* _____

The Plurals of Nouns

Here are seven rules for forming the plurals of nouns:

1. To form the plural of most nouns, add *s*.

streets   houses   cousins   keys

2. When the singular ends in *s, sh, ch, x,* or *z,* add *es*.

hisses   torches   brushes   boxes

3. When the singular ends in *o,* add *s*.

radios   stereos   sopranos   silos

Exceptions: For a few words ending in *o* with a consonant before it, add *es*: tomatoes, heroes, potatoes, echoes

4. When the singular noun ends in *y* with a consonant before it, change the *y* to *i* and add *es*.

hobby—hobbies   cry—cries   party—parties

5. For most nouns ending in *f,* add *s*. For some nouns ending in *f* or *fe,* however, change the *f* to *v* and add *es* or *s*.

roof—roofs   cuff—cuffs   shelf—shelves   half—halves

6. Some nouns are the same for both singular and plural.

moose   deer   sheep   tuna

7. Some nouns form plurals in special ways.

man—men   foot—feet   mouse—mice

Forming Plurals. Write the plural for each of the following nouns. Use a dictionary to check your work.

1. bridge _____

2. earmuff _____

3. alley _____

4. church _____

5. family _____

6. cello _____

7. moose _____

8. bench _____

9. century _____

10. life _____

Possessive Nouns

A **possessive noun** shows ownership of the noun that follows it. It shows that something belongs to a person or is a part of him or her.

>   *Judy's* talent   my *father's* hat

To form the possessive of a singular noun, add an apostrophe and *s*.

>   Judy—Judy's   father—father's   waitress—waitress's

If the plural noun ends in *s*, just add an apostrophe after the *s* to form the possessive.

>   ladies—ladies'   runners—runners'
>   customers—customers'   animals—animals'

If the plural noun does not end in *s*, add an apostrophe and write an *s* after the apostrophe.

>   children—children's   women—women's
>   men—men's   deer—deer's

Writing Possessive Forms of Nouns. Write the possessive form of each of these nouns.

1. grasshopper _____

2. Dr. Ross _____

3. teacher _____

4. builder _____

5. man _____

6. Cindy _____

7. mouse _____

8. children _____

9. author _____

10. hamsters _____

11. drivers _____

12. deer _____

13. students _____

14. athlete _____

15. women _____

Review: Using Nouns

Finding Nouns. In each sentence below, write **S** over the subject of the sentence, **D.O.** over the direct object, and **I.O.** over the indirect object.

　　　　　　　　　S　　*I.O.*　　　　*D.O.*
Example: Ted gave Elaine the wrong book.

1. The Mayor sent our school a special award.

2. Did Buddy serve the family hamburgers?

3. The assistant handed the carpenter a hammer.

4. The student should have brought the teacher a note.

5. Pete loaned Lou his umbrella.

Identifying Predicate Nouns. Underline the predicate noun in each sentence.

1. Millie is the captain of our volleyball team.

2. Such a hasty decision might be a mistake.

3. The ten-kilometre run was a challenge for us.

4. Our house is the oldest building on the block.

5. Rodney Wilkerson will be our new representative.

Forming Plurals and Possessives. In the blank at the right, form the plural or the possessive form, as directed, for each of the following nouns.

1. deer (plural) _____

2. shelf (plural) _____

3. Chris (singular possessive) _____

4. driver (plural possessive) _____

5. child (plural possessive) _____

What Are Pronouns?

A pronoun is a word used in place of a noun. Pronouns have three forms: *subject*, *object*, and *possessive*.

The *boys* cut the tree.	*They* cut the tree. (subject)
Willie thanked *Fay*.	Willie thanked *her*. (direct object)
Where is *Ed's* book?	Where is *his* book? (possessive)

Pronouns change form according to their use in the sentence. The pronouns listed below are **personal pronouns.** These are the forms you should know.

	SUBJECT	POSSESSIVE	OBJECT
SINGULAR:	I, you, she, he, it	my, mine, your, yours, her, hers, his, its	me, you, her him, it
PLURAL:	we, they	our, ours, your, yours, their, theirs	us, you, them

Using Pronouns Correctly. Rewrite the following sentences, changing all the proper nouns to pronouns.

> Example: Mary gave Chris and Harry some paper. (You are Mary; use one word for Chris and Harry.)

I gave them some paper.

1. The bike belongs to Carl. (Carl is your friend; use a word for the bike.)

_____

2. The Fishers gave Karyn a party. (You are not Karyn; use one word for the Fishers.)

_____

3. Show Vicki the program. (You are not Vicki.)

_____

4. George will give Angela the book that belongs to Angela. (You are George, and you are talking to Angela.)

_____

5. Mr. Spock handed Captain Kirk's phaser to the Martians and Venusians. (You are Captain Kirk; use one word for the creatures.)

_____

Predicate Pronouns

The subject forms of pronouns are used as subjects. They are also used as predicate pronouns. A **predicate pronoun** is a pronoun that follows a linking verb and is linked by the verb to the subject.

SUBJECTS   PREDICATE PRONOUNS
You and *I* won.   The winners were *you* and *I*.

Here are some points to remember about predicate pronouns:
 1. Predicate pronouns follow linking verbs such as *is, was, were,* and *will be.*
 2. The predicate pronoun usually means the same thing as the subject.
 3. A sentence with a predicate pronoun will usually make sense if the subject and the predicate pronoun are reversed.

He was the kicker.
The kicker was *he.*

Always use the subject form of a pronoun for subjects and predicate nouns.

INCORRECT: The runner was him.
CORRECT: The runner was *he.*

Choosing the Right Pronoun. Underline the correct form of the subject and predicate pronouns.

1. Billy and (she, her) went to the basketball game.

2. The most excited spectators were (we, us).

3. Rick and (he, him) deliver papers after school.

4. The real victim of the plot was (she, her).

5. The skaters were Jimmy and (we, us).

6. Two of the biggest fans were (he, him) and (I, me).

7. The dog trainer was (she, her).

8. Mary and (she, her) were good students.

9. The leaders will be (he, him) and (she, her).

10. The best football player was (she, her).

Possessive Forms of Pronouns 113

The possessive forms of pronouns have no apostrophes.

my, mine	our, ours
your, yours	your, yours
his, her, hers, its	their, theirs

Its and ***It's.*** Remember not to confuse the possessive pronoun *its* with the contraction *it's* (*it is* or *it has*).

> The dog lost *its* tags.
> *It's* raining again.

Using *Its* and *It's* Correctly. Underline the possessive form of the pronouns. Insert apostrophes when needed for contractions.

1. The bird prepared its nest for its young.

2. Its theirs.

3. The dog wagged its tail.

4. Since its rained for over a week, our street is flooded.

5. Its been nice to see you.

6. Is your robot able to move its arm?

7. If its warm today, we can walk to school.

8. Their newspaper was wet. Its pages were stuck together.

9. The gerbil raised its head at the noise.

10. Your cat is in our yard.

11. Orrin found his bike.

12. Our maple tree lost its leaves early in the fall.

13. Please tell us when its time to leave.

14. Polly put the dictionary back in its place.

15. Friendship is its own reward.

Pronouns as Objects

Direct objects and indirect objects always take the object form of pronouns.

DIRECT OBJECT:	Larry helped *him* and *her*.
INDIRECT OBJECT:	Sally asked *me* a question.

A compound object, either direct or indirect, may consist of two pronouns, or a noun and a pronoun, connected by *and*, *or*, or *nor*. The object form of pronouns is used in all compound objects.

DIRECT OBJECT:	Ted thanked *Terry* and *me*.
	Jean saw *her* and *him*.
INDIRECT OBJECT:	Give *Alice* and *me* a hand.
	The clerk brought *us* and *them* the forms.

Choosing the Correct Pronoun as Object. Underline the correct pronoun in each of the following sentences.

1. The soldier saluted Jimmy and (he, him).

2. When will you send (she, her) and (I, me) the report?

3. All the skiers followed (they, them) and (we, us) down the slope.

4. The shifting wind hit (she, her) from all sides.

5. Phoebe showed Patty and (we, us) the Indian arrowhead.

6. The archaeologist helped (they, them) at the dig.

7. Rick met Lois and (she, her) at the train station.

8. Please help the customers and (we, us) with our shopping.

9. The contestant answered (they, them).

10. The host greeted (he, him) and (I, me).

11. The invalid thanked (she, her) for the help.

12. My mother poured Lance and (he, him) some milk.

13. The master of ceremonies awarded Bev and (I, me) the prize.

14. Everyone in the audience saw (we, us) and the rest of the cast.

15. The stranger asked (he, him) and (she, her) for directions.

We Girls or *Us Girls*;
We Boys or *Us Boys*

When do you say *we boys* and *we girls?* When do you say *us boys* and *us girls?* You will make the correct choice if you try the pronoun alone in the sentence.

(We, Us) girls hiked along the beach.
(*We* hiked. Therefore, *We girls* hiked is correct.)

Using the Correct Pronoun. Underline the correct pronoun in each of the following sentences.

1. Give (we, us) other players a chance.

2. (We, Us) girls were chosen as monitors.

3. Mrs. Morgan gave (we, us) boys a cooking lesson.

4. After a while, (we, us) students learned the material.

5. (We, Us) campers built a bonfire.

6. Did you see (we, us) skaters in the race?

7. Did you recognize (we, us) girls in our costumes?

8. (We, Us) scientists saw an exploding star.

9. The dog followed (we, us) boys home.

10. Insiders gave (we, us) spies the information.

11. Quickly, (we, us) students set up the tables.

12. You knew (we, us) fellows immediately.

13. The police showed (we, us) reporters the proof.

14. Mother gave (we, us) all a grateful look.

15. (We, Us) players grabbed the ball and ran.

16. In a flash, (we, us) divers saw the danger.

17. Hand (we, us) swimmers our towels, please.

18. (We, Us) two were chosen as cafeteria helpers.

19. They helped (we, us) left-handers.

20. (We, Us) girls like football, too.

Pronouns and Antecedents   116

The antecedent of a pronoun is the noun or pronoun that it replaces or to which it refers. The antecedent usually appears before the pronoun, sometimes even in the sentence before it.

> The *architect* came today and brought *her* drawings.
>   (*architect* is the antecedent of *her*.)
> *Debby* and *Tom* came in. *They* were laughing.
>   (*Debby* and *Tom* are the antecedents of *They*.)

Finding the Antecedents. Underline the pronouns in each of the following sentences. Circle their antecedents and draw an arrow to them.

Example: Janice rode her bicycle.

1. The ferocious lion captured its prey.

2. Mrs. Fisher gave David his lunch.

3. The Erie Canal is used for barges. It moves them quickly.

4. Uncle Jack is driving a Fiesta. He just bought it.

5. The girl cut her finger badly.

6. Has Jim found his jacket? It is on the table.

7. Flowers open their petals in the sun.

8. Marc must carry his own backpack.

9. Where is the calculator? It is in the drawer.

10. Mandy brought her skateboard with her.

11. Carol and Sandy went their separate ways.

12. The lonely girl looked for her friend.

13. The ranchers rode their horses through the canyon.

14. Sheep care for their lambs.

15. Ms. Edelman arrived at her job.

Indefinite Pronouns 117

Some pronouns do not refer to a particular person. They are called **indefinite pronouns.** The following indefinite pronouns are singular:

another	either	nobody
anybody	everybody	no one
anyone	everyone	one
anything	everything	somebody
each	neither	someone

Because these pronouns are singular, we use the singular possessive pronouns *his, her,* or *its* to refer to them.

Everybody ate *his* dinner.
No one had *her* knapsack.

Using Indefinite Pronouns Correctly. Choose the correct possessive pronoun from the parentheses and underline it. Circle the antecedent.

Example: Someone left (her or his, their) pen here.

1. Before the test, anyone can look at (his or her, their) book.

2. Neither of the girls was in (her, their) place.

3. If everybody would do (his or her, their) work, we could be done soon.

4. Does anyone have (her, their) own flashlight?

5. Sooner or later, everyone must make (her or his, their) own decisions.

6. Somebody just moved (his, their) desk.

7. At the trial, each of the witnesses told (her or his, their) story.

8. Nobody could see (his, their) shadow in the dark.

9. Someone canceled (his, their) subscription.

10. Is there anybody who will donate (her, their) time?

11. Everybody went (her, their) own way.

12. Somebody forgot (his or her, their) books.

13. Neither of the contestants chose (her, their) best category.

14. Seldom does each of us take (his, their) time.

15. No one had (her, their) proper supplies.

Review: Using Pronouns

Using Pronouns Correctly. Underline the correct pronouns in the sentences below.

1. Everyone told (her, their) side of the story.

2. The youth club just remodeled (its, it's) recreation room.

3. Mrs. Sorkin gave Adam and (we, us) some cupcakes.

4. My uncle has made his famous chicken soup.

5. The officer and (I, me) smiled at each other.

6. (Its, It's) very foggy outside.

7. The principal watched the coach and (he, him) carefully.

8. Is everybody at (his, their) own house?

9. (We, Us) girls and (they, them) visited the nursery.

10. Cheryl took Gail and (she, her) to the movies.

11. It was (I, me) who called.

12. The hardest workers were (he, him) and (we, us) girls.

Finding the Antecedents. Underline each pronoun. Circle its antecedent and draw an arrow to it.

1. Giraffes get their supper from the trees.

2. George understood the question. He answered it correctly.

3. The toy has lost its batteries.

4. My uncle has made his famous chicken soup.

5. Musicians handle their instruments carefully.

6. Tammy made some earrings. She gave them to her mom.

7. The kids and Dad practiced. They had a good time.

8. Carol made a huge sandwich and then ate it.

What Are Adjectives?

Adjectives help to give your reader a clear picture of what you are talking about. They limit, or *modify*, the meaning of another word.

An adjective is a word that modifies a noun or a pronoun.

Adjectives can tell three different kinds of things about the words they modify:

1. *What kind: yellow* ribbon, *cold* nose, *Irish* music
2. *How many: seven* dwarfs, *some* people, *less* juice
3. *Which one or ones: this* glove, *that* pirate, *these* cameras

Finding the Adjectives. Underline the adjectives in each of the following sentences. You need not bother with *a, an,* or *the.*

1. The fluorescent fixture was an old one.

2. Older brothers often tease younger brothers.

3. Ten chocolate cupcakes were on the long narrow counter.

4. The magnificent chorus sang many songs.

5. Janet prepared an Italian dinner.

6. A dissatisfied customer told the harried manager the whole story.

7. Six furry dogs ran across the busy street.

8. Pieces of Swiss cheese were eaten by the clever mice.

9. The huge elephants trumpeted.

10. The sneaky burglar approached the empty house.

Using Adjectives. Write a clear, exact adjective in each blank.

1. The _____ car is clean.

2. The _____ baker had finished the

_____rolls and bread.

3. _____ people like _____ music.

4. A _____ gorilla walked into the

_____ cage.

5. The _____ woman carried the _____

packages.

6. The _____ men ate their food.

Predicate Adjectives

Adjectives usually come before the words they modify.

>The *old* and *tattered* doll lay at the bottom of the trunk.

Sometimes they are put after the words they modify.

>The doll, *old* and *tattered*, lay at the bottom of the trunk.

However, in some sentences adjectives are separated from the words they modify by a linking verb. These adjectives are called **predicate adjectives** because they appear in the predicate.

A predicate adjective is an adjective in the predicate that modifies the subject.

>   S   LV   PA
>The day was sunny. (*sunny* modifies *day*.)

Finding Linking Verbs and Predicate Adjectives. In each of the following sentences, underline the subject once, and the linking verb twice. Then circle the predicate adjective.

>Example: The assignment seemed easy.

1. The chipmunks were noisy.

2. Mothers sometimes seem strict.

3. Richie was tired.

4. Are jeans fashionable?

5. The forest appeared silvery in the moonlight.

6. Her face was radiant.

7. Freshly baked bread tastes good.

8. The silence seemed endless.

9. Does that musician look sleepy?

10. My dogs always appear alert.

11. I felt uncomfortable.

12. The table feels sticky.

13. Isn't that room cozy?

14. Their house looks dark without the front light.

15. Carpets from the Orient are expensive.

Pronouns Used as Adjectives

Possessive pronouns are often classed as adjectives. A possessive pronoun is a modifier because it makes the meaning of a noun more definite.

    my locker   *your* boots   *their* desks

My, your, his, her, its, our, and *their* are possessive pronouns used as adjectives.

Finding Pronouns Used as Adjectives. Draw an arrow from the possessive pronoun to the word it modifies.

1. The dog buried its bone.

2. His present was wrapped beautifully.

3. Carl's mother and father canceled their vacation.

4. Our dentist changed her schedule.

5. Several giraffes extended their necks over the fence.

6. Dr. Grayson gave my brother an examination.

7. Did you answer his question?

8. Inuits build their igloos with snow.

9. The lawn mower is old, and its blades are rusty.

10. The squirrel was frightened by my presence.

Possessive pronouns have antecedents when they are used as adjectives. They are singular if their antecedents are singular, and they are plural if their antecedents are plural.

    The boy is losing *his* voice.   The boys are losing *their* voices.

Finding the Antecedents for the Possessive Pronouns. Draw an arrow from each possessive pronoun to its antecedent.

1. Several students raised their hands.

2. Tanya lost her favorite ring at the store.

3. Wally took his model airplane to school.

4. The old house had lost its shingles.

5. Perry, your story was the best.

Adjectives in Comparisons

Adjectives can be used to compare one thing with another, or one thing with many other things.

Tom is *taller* than Terry.   Tom is the *tallest* in the class.

The form of the adjective used to compare two things is called the **comparative form** and is signaled by adding *-er* to the adjective.

Tall + er = taller

The form of the adjective used to compare three or more things is called the **superlative form** and is signaled by adding *-est* to the adjective.

Tall + -est = tallest

Adjectives ending in *y* change *y* to *i* before adding *-er* or *-est* (*easy, easier*).

Longer adjectives are usually compared by the use of *more* for the comparative form and *most* for the superlative form.

ADJECTIVE	COMPARATIVE FORM	SUPERLATIVE FORM
beautiful	more beautiful	most beautiful
special	more special	most special

A few adjectives use completely new words for the comparative and superlative forms.

good	better	best
bad	worse	worst

Using Adjectives in Comparisons. Write the correct form of the adjective in the blank.

1. Your shoes look (comparative of *new*) than mine. _____

2. Our team is the (superlative of *good*). _____

3. That test was the (superlative of *difficult*). _____

4. Susan seemed (comparative of *happy*) than Pat. _____

5. Of the two towels, this one feels (comparative of *soft*). _____

6. My birthday is (comparative of *special*) than New Years. _____

7. My cold got (comparative of *bad*). _____

8. Mr. Roper was (comparative of *cranky*) than usual. _____

9. Everybody seemed (comparative of *silent*) than usual. _____

10. It was the (superlative of *long*) night of my life. _____

Demonstrative Adjectives

The words *this*, *that*, *these*, and *those* may be used as modifiers with nouns or pronouns to point out specific things. When used as modifiers, these four words are called **demonstrative adjectives.** They tell *which one* or *which ones* about the nouns they modify.

I like *this* coat, but I don't like *that* one.

When they are used by themselves, instead of as modifiers, these words are called **demonstrative pronouns.**

I like *that*.   *This* is better.

When used as adjectives, *this* and *that* are used with singular nouns. *These* and *those* are used with plural nouns.

The nouns *kind* and *sort* are singular. We say this *kind* and this *sort*. *These kinds* and *those sorts* are plural.

Finding the Demonstrative Adjectives. Underline each demonstrative adjective. Draw an arrow to the word it modifies.

1. That arrow in the weathervane points east.

2. Do you see those kittens?

3. This picture is Karen's favorite.

4. I find these kinds of pets more appealing.

5. The candidate of that party is honest.

Using Demonstrative Adjectives. Fill in the blanks with *this kind*, *that kind*, *that sort*, *these sorts*, or *those kinds*. Check that all the words are singular, or that all the words are plural.

1. We always choose _____ of paint for our house.

2. _____ of parties always take time to plan.

3. _____ of mystery story makes me shiver.

4. I don't like _____ of jokes.

5. Please find me _____ of pen.

Review: Using Adjectives

Underline each word used as an adjective in each sentence below. Circle the word it modifies, and draw an arrow to it. Ignore *a*, *an*, and *the*.

Example: That old (car) was a classic.

1. Her curly hair appeared shiny in the sun.

2. The seven little men carried their heavy tools.

3. The rowdy, irresponsible audience ruined the show.

4. A mysterious stranger sauntered up to the bossy clerk.

5. A cloud of reddish smoke floated over the gray city.

6. The new student was shy.

7. The icy fog hung in the dirty air.

8. The little girl felt confident.

9. Many brave explorers crossed the snowy tundra.

10. That happy clown did his old, timeless tricks.

Underline the possessive pronoun in each sentence. Draw an arrow to its antecedent.

Example: The girls led their class.

1. Lee was proud of her brother.

2. Rachel and Sarah waited for their father.

3. The puppy followed its mother.

4. Daniel took his skateboard outside.

5. The flowers are opening their buds.

6. Peter's aunt gave him her old radio.

7. The shy girl gave her new friend a smile.

8. The skier turned his skis sideways.

9. A tree bends its branches toward the earth.

10. The family was on its way.

What Are Adverbs?

Adverbs are words that modify verbs, adjectives, and other adverbs.

We walked *slowly*. (adverb modifying verb)

The sky was *fairly* clear. (adverb modifying adjective)

Joe talked *rather* quietly. (adverb modifying another adverb)

Adverbs answer the questions *how? when? where?* and *to what extent?*

Finding the Adverbs. Underline each adverb. Draw an arrow from the adverb to the word it modifies.

Example: Quietly, we did our chores.

1. The guard walked cautiously into the building.

2. The girls are very graceful.

3. Few cars run smoothly.

4. He left yesterday.

5. The woman swam extremely fast.

6. Slowly, we gathered our gear.

7. Good students try hard.

8. I was so happy about my new job.

9. Some fairly old paintings were displayed.

10. That boy is rather stubborn.

11. Many people drive too fast.

12. We finally finished the work.

13. They washed the car carefully.

14. She is rather shy.

15. They ride horses often.

16. The immigrant arrived today from Europe.

17. The dog ran away.

18. That joke was not funny.

19. His speech was very long.

20. Suddenly, Trish ran out.

Adverbs in Comparisons

Most adverbs that end in *-ly* form the comparative with the word *more*. They form the superlative with the word *most*.

quickly	more quickly	most quickly
carefully	more carefully	most carefully

Some adverbs add *-er* for the comparative, and *-est* for the superlative.

soon	sooner	soonest
fast	faster	fastest

Some adverbs make their comparative and superlative forms by complete word changes.

well	better	best
much	more	most
little	less	least
far	farther	farthest

Using the Correct Forms of Adverbs. Write the correct form of the adverb on the blank.

1. That horse ran (comparative of *fast*) than the other. _____

2. She used the scissors (superlative of *carefully*). _____

3. John read the directions (comparative of *closely*) than I. _____

4. Which mason worked (superlative of *well*)? _____

5. We sang (comparative of *loud*) than before. _____

6. The gears would run (comparative of *smoothly*) if they were oiled.

_____

7. I slept (comparative of *comfortably*) yesterday. _____

8. My friends went home (comparative of *early*). _____

9. She stuck to her task (superlative of *stubbornly*). _____

10. Ralph stopped (comparative of *soon*) than the others. _____

11. The ambassador traveled (superlative of *far*). _____

12. The batter hit the ball (comparative of *hard*) than I did. _____

13. Tortoises move (comparative of *slowly*) than hares. _____

14. The story was (superlative of *much*) interesting. _____

15. Who can hold this note (superlative of *long*)? _____

Using Adjectives and Adverbs Correctly   127

To use adjectives and adverbs correctly in sentences, you must always consider what kind of verb is in the sentence, *linking* or *action*. The modifier following a linking verb is usually an adjective. The modifier following an action verb is usually an adverb.

> The children feel *bad* about their behavior. (*bad* is a predicate adjective, modifying *children*.)

> The children behaved *badly*. (*badly* is an adverb modifying the action verb *behaved*. It tells *how* the children behaved.)

The words *is, am, are, was, were, be,* and *become* are often used as linking verbs. The words *seem, feel, look, appear, smell, taste,* and *sound* are sometimes linking verbs.

Do not use two negative words in a sentence when only one is needed.

> INCORRECT: We *don't* need *no* more paint.
> CORRECT: We *don't* need any more.

Choosing the Right Modifier. Underline the correct word for each of the following sentences.

1. The boy is unhappy. He feels (bad, badly).

2. Pam writes letters (good, well).

3. Many foxes seem (sly, slyly).

4. She typed her report (neat, neatly).

5. Mules are very (stubborn, stubbornly).

6. The doughnuts tasted (good, well).

7. The garden flowers smelled (fragrant, fragrantly).

8. The team didn't have (any, no) equipment.

9. The prisoners walked (slow, slowly) back to their cells.

10. Priscilla is (beautiful, beautifully).

11. They walked into the room (quieter, more quietly) than before.

12. Didn't they give you (no, any) information?

13. The room became (silent, silently) when we walked in.

14. The television set blared (constant, constantly).

15. This candy tastes (terrible, terribly).

Review: Using Adverbs

Finding the Adverbs. Underline each adverb. Draw an arrow from the adverb to the word it modifies. Watch for double adverbs.

1. The pirate limped very slowly on his wooden leg.

2. The cookies baked by the class were quite good.

3. She copied the exercise very carefully.

4. I travel this road often.

5. Jason ate his lunch too fast.

Choosing the Right Modifier. Underline the correct word for each of the following sentences.

1. Renate smiled (bright, brightly).

2. You ran around the track (quicker, more quickly) that time.

3. We all felt (bad, badly) about the accident.

4. The dog seemed (uneasy, uneasily) about something.

5. Melanie and Ron arrived (more early, earlier) than we expected.

Adding a Suitable Modifier. Fill in the blanks with suitable modifiers.

1. The _____ horse jumped _____

_____ the ditch.

2. These snakes are _____ _____.

3. The_____ girl entered the classroom _____.

4. A_____ man approached _____.

5. My _____ book fell _____ to the floor.

What Are Prepositions?

A **preposition** is a word that stands before its object and shows the relationship between that object and another word in the sentence.

> I strolled *along* the street. (*along* is the preposition; street is its object. *Along* relates *street* to *strolled*.)

A preposition is a word that relates its object to some other word in the sentence.

Here are some words we often use as prepositions:

about	around	between	for	of	through
above	at	beyond	from	off	to
across	before	but (except)	in	on	toward
after	behind	by	inside	out	under
against	below	down	into	outside	until
along	beneath	during	like	over	up
among	beside	except	near	past	with

Remember, a preposition always has an object.

Finding the Prepositions. Underline the preposition in each of the following sentences.

1. Above my head sat the Cheshire cat.

2. The train roared through the tunnel.

3. Everything was fine before the tornado.

4. Sam went to church.

5. The fawn ran among the trees.

6. Several members of the group were late.

Finding Prepositions and Their Objects. In each sentence, underline each preposition. Then circle the object of each preposition.

Example: Put the book on the desk

1. Carol filled the grill with charcoal.

2. My father's car was parked near the curb.

3. Hundreds of people swarmed into the theater.

4. In the harbor was moored the schooner.

5. Before class, Jan showed the lizard to her teacher.

6. Maury lives down the street from Dan.

Using Nouns as Objects of Prepositions

Besides being used as subjects, direct objects, and indirect objects of verbs, nouns are also used as objects of prepositions.

The boy sat under the *tree*.
Are you going to the *party?*

Finding Nouns Used as Objects of Prepositions. Underline the preposition, and circle the noun used as its object.

Example: The groceries are in the car.

1. By the shining water stood the wigwam of Nokomis.

2. They traveled from Europe to the African coast.

3. The shack was built beside the railroad.

4. The campers dove into the water quickly.

5. I never heard about that problem.

6. During the winter, everyone slides down the slopes.

7. There is a hole in the bottom of this cup.

8. The children walked along the beach.

9. Was the mitten under the couch?

10. A few firefighters climbed up the ladders.

11. We bought a tie for Dad.

12. The pot simmered on the stove.

13. The line around the theater was very long.

14. Rumpelstiltskin was the name of the dwarf.

15. The Mackenzie is the largest of our rivers.

16. Put the packages on the counter.

17. We relaxed on the beach.

18. Isaac Newton sat beneath an apple tree.

19. The burglar looked around the room.

20. They told us about the baby's birth.

Using Pronouns as Objects of Prepositions

The object forms of pronouns are used for objects of prepositions.
The object forms to remember are *me, us, her, him, them,* and *whom.*

> Ann talked *to us.*   We thought *of him.*   Come *with me.*

Whom is the object form of the interrogative pronoun. *Who* is the subject form.

> *Who* has the key? (*Who* is the subject.)
>
> To *whom* did you give the key? (*whom* is the object of *to.*)

Sometimes the object of a preposition is compound.

> Take it to *John* and *him.*

A way to test compound objects is to say the pronoun along with the preposition. Then say it in the complete sentence.

> Take it to (he, *him*).   Take it to *John* and *him.*

Using Pronouns as Objects of Prepositions. Underline the correct pronoun from the two given in parentheses. Circle the preposition.

> Example: I gave the ring (to)(she, her).

1. The magician stared directly at Paul and (I, me).

2. Behind (we, us) sat a group of gigglers.

3. I received an invitation from (she, her).

4. The friendly dog lay beside (they, them).

5. For (who, whom) is that letter intended?

6. There's nobody here but (I, me).

7. The sweater was from my cousin and (they, them).

8. Stand behind (she, her).

9. The graduates filed past (they, them) and (I, me).

10. Behind (he, him) lay the town.

11. The plan developed among the members of the council and (we, us).

12. Lights from a car came toward (he, him) and (I, me).

13. The medals were awarded to Paul and (she, her).

14. Let's sit between (she, her) and (he, him).

15. The librarian is talking about you and (I, me).

The group of words that includes a preposition and its object is a **prepositional phrase.** Words that modify the object are also part of the phrase.

Brad found the pencils *in the big oak desk.*

If the preposition has a compound object, both are included in the prepositional phrase.

I sat *beside Gary and his father.* (*beside Gary and his father* is a prepositional phrase with a compound object.)

Finding the Prepositional Phrases. Underline the prepositional phrases in the following sentences.

Example: She gave the book to the science teacher.

1. Across the street waited the taxi.

2. There was a pile of leaves in the driveway.

3. Take this vitamin with a glass of water.

4. I found a letter inside the yellow envelope.

5. The boy came with the old man and his wife.

6. During the holidays, she will stay with us.

7. For whom is the package in the blue paper?

8. Planes flew over the trees and the houses.

9. He trudged toward town.

10. That is a joke between Louis and Gary.

11. We sang by the light of the silvery moon.

12. My friend will be ready in a minute.

13. Rabbits live in holes under the cold ground.

14. We looked at the photographs and paintings.

15. On Saturday, Debby stayed around the house.

Prepositional Phrases as Modifiers

Prepositional phrases do the same work in a sentence as adjectives and adverbs. **A phrase that modifies a noun or pronoun is an adjective phrase.**

The cover *of the book* is blue.

A phrase that modifies a verb is an adverb phrase.

The football team practiced *after school*.

Identifying Prepositional Phrases. Underline the prepositional phrase in each sentence, and circle the word it modifies. On the blank, write **adjective** or **adverb** to indicate the kind of prepositional phrase it is.

Example: The girl in the blue dress sat down. _adjective_

1. Several lamps in the room were unlit. _____

2. They walked over the bridge. _____

3. After the game, he walked home. _____

4. Books were piled on the stairs. _____

5. The smoke went up the chimney. _____

6. The man in the striped shirt is the referee. _____

7. We waited until the intermission. _____

8. Hectares of corn were ruined. _____

9. The country beyond the sea is England. _____

10. Our seats were near the fifty-yard line. _____

11. Miners found coal under the mountain. _____

12. The journey into the past was exciting. _____

13. We asked several questions about the assignment. _____

14. The young captain stood on the deck. _____

15. Larry's aunt laughed at the joke. _____

Preposition or Adverb?

A number of words that are used as prepositions are also used as adverbs.

We fell *down*. (adverb)

We fell *down* the stairs. (preposition)

When you are in doubt as to whether a word is an adverb or a preposition, see how it is used. If it introduces a phrase, it is probably a preposition. If the word is used alone, it is probably an adverb.

Identifying Prepositions and Adverbs. Tell whether the italicized word in each sentence below is used as a preposition or an adverb.

Examples: He had never seen the girl *before*. _____ *adverb* _____

He had never seen the girl *before* class. *preposition*

1. The officer looked *around*. _____

2. The officer looked *around* the room. _____

3. I ran *out* the door. _____

4. I ran *out* quickly. _____

5. Please come *inside* soon. _____

6. Please come *inside* the house. _____

7. The firefighters slid *down* and ran to the trucks. _____

8. The firefighters slid *down* the pole. _____

9. Papers were thrown *about*. _____

10. Papers were thrown *about* my room. _____

11. Our friends stopped *by*. _____

12. Our friends stopped *by* our booth. _____

13. *Beyond* the barricade lay freedom. _____

14. *Beyond* lay freedom. _____

15. They finally got *outside* the auditorium. _____

16. They finally got *outside*. _____

17. Attendants stood *near*, ready to help. _____

18. Attendants stood *near* the surgeon. _____

19. We watched the geese fly *over* the lake. _____

20. We watched the geese fly *over* in formation. _____

Beginning Sentences with Prepositional Phrases

For the sake of emphasis, we sometimes begin a sentence with a prepositional phrase. Also, beginning this way will add interest to your writing.

> We arrived at the station in the morning.
> In the morning, we arrived at the station.

It is not necessarily better to start a sentence with a prepositional phrase. A variety of sentence beginnings makes more interesting reading.

Beginning Sentences with Prepositional Phrases. Rewrite the following sentences so that each begins with a prepositional phrase. If the phrase is a long one, place a comma after it.

1. We will get off the train at the next stop.

   _____

2. Police surrounded the building in a matter of minutes.

   _____

3. The air smelled fresh on that wonderful winter morning.

   _____

4. The girls bought some popcorn during the intermission.

   _____

5. Birds sang sweetly after the rainfall.

   _____

6. The excited crowd roared during the final inning.

   _____

7. Several people fainted inside the hot, stuffy room.

   _____

8. We toured the art gallery on the last day of our vacation.

   _____

9. Linda tripped and fell in the middle of her routine.

   _____

10. Steve walked home slowly after the exhausting game.

   _____

Placement of Prepositional Phrases

Sometimes a prepositional phrase may be moved from one position to another in a sentence without changing the meaning. At other times, however, the position of a prepositional phrase makes a great deal of difference in the meaning of a sentence.

INCORRECT: The store opens on the corner at 9:00.

CORRECT: The store on the corner opens at 9:00.

Using Prepositional Phrases Correctly. Rewrite the following sentences by changing the position of one prepositional phrase to make the meaning clearer.

1. With long ears and an orange wig the child laughed at the clown.

_____

2. We took photographs of the sea on the pier.

_____

3. Sandy told jokes to the class about horses.

_____

4. The teacher kept his class after school on the second floor.

_____

5. Susan mailed the letter to her grandmother in the post office.

_____

6. Harry left his books on the bus in his hurry.

_____

7. Alice told us about the great vacation she had at lunch.

_____

8. The girl sang her solo for the second time in the chorus.

_____

9. The ice cream is for dessert in the freezer.

_____

10. A cat appeared at our door with long white fur.

_____

What Are Conjunctions?

A conjunction is a word that connects words or groups of words.

Coordinating conjunctions join only words or groups of words that are of equal importance. Coordinating conjunctions are *and, but,* and *or.* Most words or groups of words joined by coordinating conjunctions are called compound constructions.

> Ken *read* and *reviewed* the chapter. (*and* connects *read* and *reviewed,* forming a compound verb.)
>
> Her letter was *short* but *interesting.* (*but* connects *short* and *interesting,* compound predicate adjectives.)
>
> Your books are on the *counter* or the *table.* (*or* connects *counter* and *table,* compound objects of the preposition *on.*)

Using Compound Constructions. Underline the compound construction in each of the following sentences. Circle the conjunction.

> Example: Two eager <u>students</u> and their <u>teacher</u> planned the fair.

1. My pen and pencil are missing.

2. John hopped and skipped in the relay race.

3. The Argonauts or the Tiger Cats will probably win the division title.

4. The typing students hunt and peck for the keys.

5. The fish flipped and flopped in the net.

6. You can choose the black checkers or the red ones.

7. Mario and Anna went to the soccer game.

8. The doctor quickly but carefully took charge.

9. I never saw Aunt Matilda or Uncle Harold.

10. Joe watched and waited for the bus.

11. I am hungry and thirsty.

12. The reporter listened and learned.

13. The travelers waited for a plane or a train.

14. The toys on the table and the floor are broken.

15. Proof was needed and was found.

Review: Using Prepositions and Conjunctions 138

Finding the Prepositional Phrases. Underline each prepositional phrase in each of the following sentences. Circle the object (or objects) of the preposition. On the blank, write **adjective** if the phrase is an adjective prepositional phrase, or **adverb** if the phrase is an adverb prepositional phrase.

Example: The girl with the braces smiled. _adjective_

1. A bloodhound sniffed around the garage. _____

2. Everybody inside the cabin was a suspect. _____

3. Mr. Jones was a witness for the prosecution. _____

4. The left side of the bleachers needs repair. _____

5. Mary usually sits with Ellen and her. _____

Identifying Prepositions and Adverbs. Is the word in italics a **preposition** or an **adverb?** Write your answer on the blank.

1. The ship went *down* fast. _____

2. *Under* no circumstances should you leave. _____

3. We looked *inside*, but the room was empty. _____

4. The child climbed *out* the window. _____

5. May we come *along*, too? _____

Using Compound Constructions. Underline the compound construction in each of the following sentences. Circle the conjunction.

1. The bus driver stopped quickly but carefully.

2. Mary or Marlene will be president of the class.

3. Burt Reynolds and Sally Field are in that movie.

4. Weston read a book about stamps and coins.

5. Was the message for him or me?

What Are Compound Sentences? 139

A *simple sentence* is a sentence with only one subject and one predicate. Both the subject and the predicate may be compound.

A compound sentence consists of two or more simple sentences joined together. The parts of a compound sentence may be joined by a coordinating conjunction (*and, but, or*) or by a semicolon (;).

> We earned nine dollars, **and** we put it in the bank.
> The sun was up; the morning beckoned.

Using compound sentences helps to make your writing more interesting and readable.

Analyzing Compound Sentences. Underline the subject once and the verb twice in each part of the compound sentence; circle the conjunction.

> Example: I saw the light, (and) I followed it.

1. He went to the store, but Jody went home.

2. Either she is in court, or she is at her office.

3. The show ended, and we left.

4. The phone rang several times, but nobody answered.

5. Greg shoveled the snow, and his brother watched him.

6. We can play Scrabble, or we can read.

7. Lawyers argue cases, but judges decide them.

8. We had a puppy, but it ran away.

9. Fred clutched at the brake, and the bike stopped just in time.

10. Everyone played, but Jenny scored the winning basket.

11. The clown smiled, and the child blushed.

12. Either you walk to school, or you take the bus.

13. Kathy called, but nobody was home.

14. The spaceship landed; the journey was over.

15. He has no problems, but he worries anyway.

Compound Predicate or Compound Sentence? 140

You will often need to know the difference between a compound sentence and a simple sentence with a compound predicate.

> Tony *washed the dishes* and *dried them*.
>> (This is a simple sentence. The conjunction *and* joins two parts of a compound predicate.)
>
> Tony *washed the dishes,* and *I dried them*.
>> (This is a compound sentence. The conjunction *and* joins two simple sentences, each with its own subject and verb.)

Identifying Compound Predicates and Compound Sentences. Decide whether the following sentences are compound sentences or simple sentences with compound predicates. For each, write either **CS** (compound sentence) or **CP** (compound predicate) in the blank.

1. The student raised his hand and answered the question. _____

2. They gathered the food, and we distributed it. _____

3. His father went to the auto show, but Jeff stayed home. _____

4. Did you walk or ride your bike? _____

5. Several people listened, but nobody volunteered. _____

6. John and Jane got home early and started supper. _____

7. Our team won the game, and everyone cheered. _____

8. The train slowed down and sounded its whistle. _____

9. You can stay home or go to the movies. _____

10. The foolish fox ate greedily, but the cunning crow just watched. _____

11. Beth broke her leg, but she didn't cry. _____

12. Tom and Gail liked the pie but couldn't finish it. _____

13. He could hit the puck or skate with it. _____

14. It rained, but I went anyway. _____

15. The squirrel found the nut and buried it. _____

Commas in Compound Constructions

Since compound sentences are made up of two or more simple sentences, they may be long. To help the reader keep the thoughts in order, put a comma before the coordinating conjunction in a compound sentence.

Tarzan swung through the trees, and his chimp followed.

Do not use a comma to separate two direct objects, two predicates, or two of any other compound constructions.

The Tiger team and the Lion team tied for second place.

Finally, the comma is not necessary in a very short compound sentence.

We waited.and we waited.

Punctuating Compound Constructions. In the following sentences, commas have been omitted from all the compound constructions. Put commas where needed. If the sentence is correct, write **c** after it.

Example: I ate two bags of peanuts, and I got a stomachache. _____

1. Our school play is tonight and we are somewhat nervous. _____

2. A white stallion and his band of horses roamed the hills. _____

3. He was hiding in the jungle but they did not see him. _____

4. We could follow that path or start out on a new one. _____

5. Sam bought a hat but he needed a new shirt. _____

6. The auction started and I bought three comics. _____

7. Other questions were raised but the scientist ignored them. _____

8. The thermometer registered seventy but still the boy was cold. _____

9. Susan could become a doctor or she could be a lawyer. _____

10. Shooting stars lit up the sky and fell from sight. _____

11. Our dog lay on the couch and slept peacefully. _____

12. The eggs were done perfectly but the bacon was burned. _____

13. George opened his eyes at once and looked up at the ceiling. _____

14. He knew the solution but for a minute he was mixed up. _____

15. She could saddle her horse or she could ride bareback. _____

Combining Related Thoughts   142

We have said that a compound sentence consists of two or more simple sentences joined together. However, the simple sentences must be related in thought if they are combined into a compound sentence.

UNRELATED: Patricia rode her bike. My bike has a flat tire.
RELATED: Patricia rode her bike, *but* I had to walk.

Some pairs of sentences make good compound sentences, and some do not. They must be related in thought.

Making Compound Sentences. Find the six sentence pairs that might be made into compound sentences. Rewrite them, using a comma and a coordinating conjunction. Four pairs should not be combined.

1. Renee enjoyed seeing her old friends at the party. She wore her new jeans.

_____

2. We could go bowling. We could go to a movie.

_____

3. The Prime Minister will sign the bill. He might wait a week.

_____

4. Jumbo jets are built for comfort. The plane flew among the clouds.

_____

5. The brothers played Monopoly. Dad came home early.

_____

6. Leaves fell from the trees. I sat alone in the room.

_____

7. The cars were wrecked. The passengers were unharmed.

_____

8. You can make a standing mobile that has little movement. You can make a hanging mobile that has lots of motion.

_____

_____

9. Keith completed the test. He forgot to write his name on it.

_____

10. Many castles were built in the Middle Ages. Some still exist.

_____

Review: Compound Sentences

Identifying Compound Sentences. In each of the following sentences, circle the conjunction. Underline each subject once and each verb or verb combination twice. Punctuate any compound sentences properly.

Example: We landed at the airport, and we were met by our cousins.

1. Yesterday Greg played baseball but today he is staying home.

2. The committee considered the plan and voted on it.

3. We visited Canada's Wonderland and we had a great time.

4. Janet and her cousin learned karate.

5. Soon the parade was over and the people went home.

6. The Hatfields and the McCoys were feuding but the Horners and the Shipleys kept the peace.

7. You could invest in this stock or you could buy a bond.

8. Snow fell and the world looked white.

9. Cigarettes are dangerous but some people do not care.

10. We bought some flowers and we gave them to Ms. Wallace.

Using Compound Constructions. In the following sentences, the compound constructions are incomplete. Complete them. Remember that a comma is used in compound sentences.

1. The dictionary and _____ lay on the table.

2. Dr. Harris gave me the shot and _____

3. My dad bought a moped, and _____

4. He peeled the potatoes and _____

5. We could go fishing, or _____

6. Stacy saw the U.F.O., but _____

7. The kids will eat the popcorn and _____

8. The raft ran the rapids and _____

9. The dance was fun but _____

10. Frances wrote a letter, but _____

Agreement of Subject and Verb   **144**

A singular subject must have a singular verb. A plural subject must have a plural verb.

The *cats* (plural) *were* (plural) scratching the pillow.

He (singular) *has* (singular) a cold.

Here are some important things to remember:

1. A prepositional phrase may appear between the subject and the verb. Look only at whether the subject is singular or plural when you choose your verb.

Each (of the houses) *was* brown.   *One* (of the clocks) *doesn't* work.

Many *barrels* (of oil) *were* shipped.   The *gears* (in this motor) *don't* mesh.

2. The pronoun *you* is never used with a singular verb. It is always used with plural verbs.

You were very helpful.   *You understand* the problem.

3. Here are special forms of certain verbs that you must know:

SINGULAR		PLURAL	
is, was	does (doesn't)	are, were	do (don't)
has		have	

Making the Subject and Verb Agree. Underline the correct form. If there is a prepositional phrase between the subject and verb, circle it.

1. The glass in the mirror (is, are) badly scratched.

2. Several people (was, were) coughing.

3. Mary (doesn't, don't) understand the problem.

4. Special moments from a vacation (means, mean) a great deal.

5. Those light bulbs on the dresser (seems, seem) frosted.

6. Each year in your life (flies, fly) by quickly.

7. You (was, were) late for lunch.

8. Some of the hospitals (has, have) visiting hours for children.

9. The house with four bedrooms (was, were) sold quickly.

10. The rug on the wall (feels, feel) soft.

11. A committee on solar heat (deals, deal) with energy problems.

12. The energy from coal (keeps, keep) us warm this winter.

13. Our policy in these matters (is, are) a fair one.

14. The remarks by the President (was, were) misquoted.

15. He (doesn't, don't) want to hurt anyone's feelings.

Verbs with Compound Subjects   145

A compound subject is two or more subjects used with the same verb. A compound subject that contains the conjunction *and* is plural; therefore, the plural verb must be used with it.

> Lettie and Brenda *are* friends. (The compound subject is *Lettie and Brenda.* The verb *are* is plural.)

When the parts of a compound subject are joined by *or* or *nor*, the verb agrees with the nearer subject.

> Neither Bob nor his sisters *are* home.
>
> The older boys or Tim *is* responsible for this work.

Using the Right Verb with a Compound Subject. Underline the correct form of the verb from the two given in parentheses.

1. Kerosene or other solvents (causes, cause) this pollution.

2. Mr. Brill and the other people (has, have) a solution.

3. Neither Sally nor her brothers (is, are) home.

4. (Do, Does) the green shirt and the blue jacket go together?

5. Warm sunny days and cool nights (helps, help) grapes grow.

6. The freshness or the flavor (is, are) missing.

7. (Do, Does) Jane or Judy have an extra notebook?

8. Cows and other barnyard animals (eats, eat) large amounts of grain.

9. Several boys and an old man (was, were) waiting for the bus.

10. The bullfighter and the bull (stares, stare) at each other.

11. (Is, Are) Dennis and Denise twins?

12. Neither guns nor a single sword (stops, stop) the musketeers.

13. Mozart and Haydn (was, were) composers of music.

14. Jill and her old friends (meets, meet) once a month.

15. (Do, Does) the pigs and the chickens get along?

16. Clay necklaces or a papier-mâché mobile (is, are) fun to make.

17. Alligators and crocodiles (looks, look) alike.

18. My parents and my teacher (agrees, agree).

19. Neither a parachute nor an ejector seat (is, are) totally safe.

20. Caterpillars or a colorful butterfly (fascinates, fascinate) me.

Agreement in Inverted Sentences   146

In most sentences, the subject comes before the verb. "The long-lost *key* was in my pocket." For emphasis, however, a writer or speaker might say, "In my pocket was the long-lost *key*." The second sentence is called an **inverted sentence** because the subject of the sentence and its verb have changed positions. In inverted sentences, as in ordinary ones, the subject and verb must agree.

Using the Right Verb in Inverted Sentences. Underline the correct form of the verb for each sentence.

1. Between Janice and me (sits, sit) the little dog.

2. At the door (was, were) my cousins.

3. Along the river (wanders, wander) the prospectors.

4. By the shores of Lake Ontario (stands, stand) many modern buildings.

5. Out of the thicket (flies, fly) the mallard.

6. Against the side of the house (leans, lean) the tired painter.

7. Above our heads (twinkle, twinkles) the stars.

8. Into the distance (rides, ride) the Lone Ranger.

9. Underneath the brush (is, are) the pine cones.

10. Down the pole (slides, slide) the firefighters.

11. On the banquet table (was, were) delicious cakes and pies.

12. Near the palace (marches, march) the guard.

13. Through kilometres of forest (thunders, thunder) the trains.

14. Behind her mother (hides, hide) the child.

15. After the elephants (comes, come) the monkeys.

16. With our congratulations (goes, go) our best wishes.

17. Inside the front page (is, are) the index.

18. Over the stadium (floats, float) a balloon.

19. Outside the circle (stands, stand) a group of men.

20. Around the room (fly, flies) the parakeets.

Verbs with *There*

As you may remember, *there* is often used to get a sentence going. The subject is farther on in the sentence. When *there* is used at the beginning of a sentence, be careful to make the verb of the sentence agree in number with the real subject of the sentence.

> There *is* a *fly* in my soup. (The verb is singular because the subject *fly* is singular.)
>
> *Are* there any *shovels* around? (The verb is plural because the subject *shovels* is plural.)

Using the Correct Verb with *There.* Underline the correct verb.

1. There (was, were) many mountain climbers in Banff.

2. Yesterday, there (was, were) a student council meeting.

3. (Is, Are) there more delegates to the convention?

4. There (is, are) several stories in this magazine.

5. There (is, are) a special gift for my family.

6. (Wasn't, Weren't) there two peanut butter sandwiches on the counter?

7. Soon there (was, were) ten rabbits in the box.

8. (Is, Are) that contestant a friend of yours?

9. There (isn't, aren't) many antique cars around.

10. There (was, were) a few late arrivals.

11. (Was, Were) there a crowd at the rock concert?

12. Last week there (was, were) a forest fire in Manitoba.

13. There (isn't, aren't) too much damage.

14. There (is, are) Anne Murray, my favorite singer.

15. In the distance, there (is, are) the outline of a city.

16. (Was, Were) there anything left from the sale?

17. (Isn't, Aren't) you excited?

18. On that shelf, there (is, are) several records by Glenn Gould.

19. There (was, were) one problem with the machine.

20. (Is, Are) there any volunteers?

Review: Making Subjects and Verbs Agree

Making Subjects and Verbs Agree. Underline the correct verb.

1. Stephanie and her father (play, plays) baseball.

2. There (was, were) one leprechaun who lost his gold.

3. Upon the hill (stands, stand) the giant willow tree.

4. Don and Bob (was, were) tennis partners.

5. Three apples and one orange (does, do) not make a fruit salad.

6. The roller coaster in the amusement park (sounds, sound) thrilling.

7. There (was, were) no stars out that night.

8. Thatched huts and concrete buildings (contrasts, contrast) greatly.

9. Each of the animals (has, have) gotten proper care.

10. All of the experts (has, have) given an opinion.

11. Neither you nor Beth (appears, appear) nervous.

12. (Is, Are) there any good cartoons on television?

13. In the book, General Crerar and his troops (invades, invade) the French seaport of Dieppe.

14. Where (was, were) you yesterday?

15. There (is, are) two birch trees by the road.

16. Through a crack in the wall (peers, peer) a mouse.

17. Either Gil or Bob (is, are) the drummer.

18. The class with the best attendance (is, are) the winner.

19. (Do, Does) every record have a cover?

20. All over his arm (swarms, swarm) the mosquitoes.

21. (Wasn't, Weren't) there any other decorations?

22. My older sisters or my dad usually (cooks, cook) dinner.

23. Either the dentist or her assistants (prepares, prepare) the patient.

24. Through the treetops (shine, shines) the moon.

25. The potatoes in the pot (is, are) mashed.

Proper Nouns and Adjectives (I)   149

Capitalize proper nouns and proper adjectives.

A **proper noun** is the name of a particular person, place, or thing.

    Sandra   Moose Jaw   Bank of Montreal   Alberta

A **common noun** is the name of a whole class of persons, places, or things. It is not capitalized.

    girl   city   continent   language

A **proper adjective** is an adjective formed from a proper noun.

    English   French   American   Spanish

Using Capital Letters Correctly. Supply capital letters where needed in the following sentences.

    Example: We visited the chocolate factory in montreal, quebec.

1. My cousins live in edmonton.

2. We studied australia and its people.

3. Is caroline from kelowna, british columbia?

4. I hope glenn michibita wins the tennis tournament.

5. James and julie visited england.

6. The romans had chariot races.

7. The citizens of oshawa voted against the law.

8. Some swedish crystal is very expensive.

9. Van gogh was a dutch painter who moved to france.

10. When did you learn hebrew?

11. Marie plays the french horn.

12. Arthur conan doyle wrote stories about sherlock holmes.

13. Does your sister attend waterloo university?

14. A gondola is a boat used in venice, italy.

15. Steven and karyn asked for italian dressing.

16. My favorite canadian artist is william kurelek.

17. Have you ever visited toronto?

18. Fred and terry attended the game.

19. The game will be played in north battleford, saskatchewan.

20. The capital of canada is ottawa.

Proper Nouns and Adjectives (II)

Names of Persons. The names and titles of specific persons, including initials or abbreviations standing for their names or titles, are capitalized.

> Martin S. Franks, Jr.   Dr. Carol Smith   Bob McAdoo

Capitalize titles of people and groups whose rank is very important.

> The Premier of Alberta attended the conference.
> The Prime Minister introduced the Speaker of the House.

Family Relationships. Words like *mother*, *father*, *aunt*, and *uncle* are capitalized when they are used as names.

> Has Dad made dinner?   My father visited Aunt Louise at her office.

The Pronoun *I*. Capitalize the pronoun, *I*.

> Did you see what I saw?

The Deity. Capitalize all words referring to the Deity, to the Holy Family, and to religious scriptures.

> God   the Gospel   the Father   Jesus   the Talmud

Using Capital Letters Correctly. Supply capital letters where needed in the following sentences.

1. The speaker of the house and the prime minister conferred.

2. When will aunt martha and uncle joe be here?

3. Do i have to see dr. sampson at his office?

4. A canadian surgeon named dr. norman bethune is well known in china.

5. Rich gossage and albert lyle also have nicknames.

6. I live in montreal, my sister lives in kitchener.

7. Christmas is the celebration of the birth of jesus.

8. Is mother upstairs, or did she go to pick up dad?

9. The man in uniform is major alan burrows.

10. Dr. martin luther king, jr. preached the gospel.

11. Grace kelly became princess Grace of Monaco.

12. Mary and i saw wayne gretsky play hockey.

13. Did you give aunt tess and uncle bill their presents?

14. The award was presented to mr. richard thomas and ms. irene samuels.

15. Did barbara frum host that show?

Geographical Names

In a geographical name, capitalize the first letter of each word except articles and prepositions.

The article *the* before a geographical name is not part of that name and is not capitalized.

> CONTINENTS: North America, Asia
> BODIES OF WATER: the Indian Ocean, the Baltic Sea, Hudson's Bay
> LAND FORMS: Canadian Rockies, Mesabi Range, Canadian Shield
> POLITICAL UNITS: York County, Township of Whitchurch/Stouffville
> PUBLIC AREAS: Algonquin Park, Fort Henry, Brock's Monument
> ROADS AND HIGHWAYS: Yonge Street, Highway 401, Canso Causeway

Capitalize names of sections of the country but not of directions of the compass. Capitalize proper adjectives derived from sections of the country. Do not capitalize words indicating direction.

> Have you ever visited the *West*?   We traveled *east* toward Ottawa.
> Our house is *west* of town.   Bruce attended an *Eastern* school.

Using Capital Letters Correctly. Supply capital letters where needed in the following sentences.

1. Our group saw niagara falls, located in ontario.

2. On our trip to the west we saw the rockies.

3. Charles Lindbergh flew his plane to an airport in france.

4. He took off from toronto international airport.

5. The immigrants traveled westward to reach manitoba.

6. The group traveled north from kamloops to prince george.

7. Highway 401 connects windsor and montreal.

8. The atlantic ocean borders dartmouth.

9. Fishing draws a lot of visitors to saint john, new brunswick.

10. We read about the montreal canadiens in *sportsweek*.

11. It is six kilometres east of highway 48.

12. The south fought the north in the war.

13. We crossed portage avenue and walked down main.

14. The old house stood on lester street.

15. The rideau canal runs through ottawa.

Other Rules for Capitalization (I)   152

Capitalize the names of organizations and institutions.

Sony Corporation	Scott Junior High School	Bank of Montreal
St. Michaels Hospital	Ontario Blue Cross	Seven-Up Company

Do not capitalize such words as *school*, *church*, *college*, and *hospital* when they are not used as names.

Capitalize the names of historical events, documents, and periods of time.

World War I	Constitutional Act
Civil War	Renaissance

Capitalize the names of months, days, and holidays.

November	Memorial Day	Wednesday
Saturday	New Year's Eve	Thanksgiving

Using Capital Letters Correctly. Supply capital letters where needed in the following sentences.

1. Cupid is a symbol of valentine's day, celebrated on february 14.

2. Labor day is the first monday in september.

3. The maple leafs and the montreal canadiens were in the playoffs.

4. The university of laval is in quebec.

5. The game will be played on new year's day.

6. We go to markham high school.

7. On november 11, we celebrate remembrance day.

8. She is a member of the organization called voice of women.

9. King john of england signed the magna carta during the middle ages.

10. We went to the museum of science and industry on friday.

11. In october, we celebrate thanksgiving.

12. When is national book week?

13. The third sunday in june is father's day.

14. Ms. Cummings works for general motors.

15. The headquarters of the united nations are located in new york city.

Other Rules for Capitalization (II)   153

Languages, Races, Nationalities, Religions. Capitalize the names of languages, races, nationalities, and religions, and also adjectives derived from them.

     Catholicism   Swiss cheese   English class

Ships, Trains, Airplanes, Automobiles. Capitalize all proper names of ships, trains, airplanes, and automobiles.

     Orient Express   Chevrolet   Lusitania

Abbreviations. Abbreviations are shortened forms of words and, if they are abbreviations of proper nouns or proper adjectives, they are capitalized.

     Capitalize the abbreviations **B.C.** and **A.D.**, and **A.M.** and **P.M.**

Using Capital Letters Correctly. Supply capital letters where needed in the following sentences.

1. Jacques Cartier was born in a.d. 1491.

2. Our family loves french cooking.

3. My grandmother sailed on the *queen mary* a long time ago.

4. The *concorde* will leave promptly at 9:00 a.m.

5. Ms. Kinzie has bought a ford fiesta.

6. Come for supper at 5:30 p.m.

7. The troupe of chinese acrobats is performing at the stadium.

8. My sister just got a siamese cat.

9. Can mayor lastman speak english, french, and chinese?

10. Charles Lindbergh flew the *spirit of st. louis.*

11. The native religion of japan is shintoism.

12. Did you buy any english china?

13. In the mystery, the watch was broken at 9:03 a. m.

14. My house looks like a spanish ranch.

15. On Sunday, the reverend john cannon gave a good sermon.

First Words (I)

Capitalize the first word of every sentence.
Capitalize the first word in most lines of poetry.

> Through the revolving door
> Of a department store
> There slithered an alligator.

Sometimes, especially in modern poetry, the lines of a poem do not begin with a
a capital letter.

Quotations. Capitalize the first word of a direct quotation, the *exact* words of
the speaker or writer.

> Mother asked, "Have you seen my umbrella?"

An **indirect quotation,** in which the words of the speaker are changed to other
words, does *not* begin with a capital letter.

> Mother asked if we had seen her umbrella.

A **divided quotation** is a direct quotation interrupted by explanatory words like
she said. The second part of this kind of quotation does not begin with a capital
letter.

> "After school," she said, "we can go to the library."

If the second part of the quotation starts a new sentence, the second part begins
with a capital letter.

> "That's it," said Tony. "That's the answer."

Using Capital Letters Correctly. Supply capital letters wherever
needed.

1. "after lunch," said Paul, "let's walk uptown."

2. "The time has come," the Walrus said,
   "to talk of many things:
   of shoes—and ships—and sealing wax—
   of cabbages—and kings."

3. my teacher told me to study hard.

4. "study hard," said my teacher. "you will do better."

5. joanie shouted, "here comes the parade!"

6. the doctor said that Dad should rest.

7. the man went to court. he was a lawyer.

8. the rhino is a homely beast,
   for human eyes he's not a feast.

First Words (II)

Letters. Capitalize the first word, words like *Sir* or *Madam*, and the name of the person addressed in the greeting of a letter.

Dear Sir or Madam: Dear Dr. Barnes:

In the complimentary close, capitalize the first word only.

Sincerely yours,   Yours very truly,

Outlines. Capitalize the first word of each line of an outline.

    I. Solar Energy
        A. Collection of heat
            1. By air
            2. By water
        B. Use of energy

Titles. Capitalize the first word and all important words in the titles of books, poems, short stories, articles, newspapers, magazines, plays, motion pictures, television programs, works of art, and musical compositions.

The words *a, an,* and *the* are not capitalized unless they come at the beginning of a title. The same is true for conjunctions and prepositions (*and, of*).

    Sports Illustrated   *A Wrinkle in Time*
    "The Raven"   *Island of the Blue Dolphins*

Using Capital Letters Correctly. Supply capital letters wherever needed.

1. The paper boy just delivered my copy of the *stouffville tribune*.

2. dear mr. samuels: I would like to order a subscription to *consumer reports*.

3. very truly yours,

4. Is "friendly giant" still on television?

5. One of my favorite poems is "the settlers" by Margaret Atwood.

6. John will sing "it's not easy being green" at the concert.

7. I have just finished reading *anne of green gables*.

8. My subscription of *canadian automotive* has expired.

9. Be sure to read "what's cool for school" in your copy of *dynamite*.

10. We're going to see *the sound of music* at the high school.

Review: Capitalization

Using Capital Letters Correctly. Supply capital letters wherever needed in the following sentences.

1. one of my favorite movies is *meatballs*.

2. an obi is a wide sash worn with a japanese kimono.

3. the blue jays are trying for their third win.

4. "next week," he said, "we leave for florida."

5. "did you enjoy the play?" asked ms. fenwick.

6. "yes," answered the class. "it was really good."

7. hold fast to dreams
   for if dreams die
   life is a broken-winged bird
   that cannot fly.

8. north america lies between the atlantic ocean and the pacific ocean.

9. dr. robbins is presenting the award to professor schwartz this evening.

10. i love german potato salad.

11. "hello," said bob. "are mom and dad here?"

12. the old testament is a collection of religious writings.

13. I. how to train your dog
    A. kinds of tricks
       1. roll over
       2. play dead
    B. kinds of rewards

14. during the middle ages, robin hood fought for king richard.

15. thanksgiving is my favorite holiday.

16. we will meet you at union station at 9:00 a.m.

17. have you read the book *jake and the kid* by w.o. mitchell?

18. a very rare comic book is *action comics #1*, published in june, 1938.

19. gordon lightfoot won a juno award.

20. our class may visit springfield next year.

The Period

Use a period at the end of a declarative sentence.

> Joe walks the dog.

A declarative statement is often shortened to one or two words in answering a question.

> What's new? Nothing. (*Nothing is new.*)

Use a period at the end of an imperative sentence.

> Please turn off the television set.

Use a period at the end of an indirect question.

> Cindy asked how much the dress was.

Use a period after an abbreviation or an initial.

> Mon. (*Monday*)   C. P. Snow   A. D. (*Anno Domini*)

Periods are omitted in some abbreviations, such as *rpm*, *km/h*, or *UN*. If you're not sure, use your dictionary.

Use a period after each number or letter that shows a division of an outline or that precedes an item in a list.

> I. Vegetables   1. clean room
>   A. Kinds   2. mow lawn
>   B. Growing season   3. call Pat

Using Periods Correctly. Supply the missing punctuation wherever needed.

1. The train passed Winnipeg, Man, on its way to Regina, Sask

2. My doctor's appointment is Tues, Dec 15 at 4:00 P M

3. Ms Nora Simpson, Dr Steven A Davis, and F D Schwartz went to the convention in Waterloo, Ont

4. A Y Jackson was one of the Group of Seven

5. Everyone asked him to stay

6. Cotton and other fiber crops were grown

7. The speed limit is 100 km/h on the highway

8. Mrs Ellison works for W H Plastic & Metal Co Ltd

9. Eat your dinner

10. We traveled to PEI before going home.

The Question Mark and the Exclamation Point

Use a question mark at the end of an interrogative sentence, a sentence that asks a question.

Where are you going?

This is a direct question, one that gives the exact words of the person who is asking. A question mark is used only with a direct question.

Do not use a question mark with an indirect question. Use a period.

Ms. Lawrence asked me if I would help.

Use an exclamation point at the end of a sentence that expresses strong feeling.

What a huge gorilla that was!

An exclamation point is also used at the end of an imperative sentence that expresses excitement or emotion.

Stop that car!

Most imperative sentences, however, are followed by a period.

Use an exclamation point after an interjection or any other exclamatory expression. An **interjection** is a word or group of words used to express strong feeling.

Wow! Oh! Ouch!

Avoid using the exclamation mark too often.

Using Question Marks and Exclamation Points Correctly. Supply the missing punctuation marks where needed. Watch for indirect questions.

1. Where were you when the lights went out

2. Wow That was a great movie

3. Help Hurry

4. Mr. Jones inquired about my health

5. Is the bank closed today

6. Watch out for flying glass

7. Was that the Lone Ranger

8. Susan asked if you knew her aunt

9. Look Do you see those lights

10. How are you feeling

The Comma (I)

Commas show a reader which words go together. They also show the reader where to pause so he or she will not be confused.

> At night time seems to pass slowly.
> After running the dogs were tired.

These sentences would be much clearer with the addition of commas.

> At night, time seems to pass slowly.
> After running, the dogs were tired.

Using Commas To Avoid Confusion. Add commas to the following sentences to make the meaning clear.

1. Inside the wall was crumbled and broken.

2. As he watched four soldiers came in after him.

3. While lighting the fire Michelle burned her fingers.

4. When he looked underneath the table seemed broken.

5. Instead of just watching my sister played the game.

6. From Paul Steven got a walkie-talkie.

7. Before resting the guard checked the building.

8. He stood with his feet apart his fists on his hips.

9. We ordered our meal and our waitress brought it in.

10. At two people filled the theater.

11. The list contained fourteen pages four cartoons and two drawings.

12. Before long alligators may be extinct.

13. When I finished cooking my father came home.

14. As they left the writer started to work again.

15. Until the thief climbed in the man thought he was safe.

16. Sorry I lost my place.

17. In the morning dew covered the ground.

18. After Margaret left the meeting was adjourned.

19. By half-past twelve six accountants had finished their work.

20. In the evening shadows appeared.

The Comma (II)

Use a comma after every item in a series except the last. These items may be nouns, verbs, modifiers, phrases, or other parts of the sentence.

> The dog barked, jumped, and rolled over. (verbs)
>
> Sam, Susan, Steve, and Scott went home. (nouns)

Use commas after the adverbs *first, second, third,* and so on.

> Check these two things: first, find your notebook; second, make sure that you have paper.

When two or more adjectives precede a noun, use a comma after each adjective except the last one.

> The forlorn, hungry dog followed us home.

When two adjectives are used together to express a single idea, commas are not used.

> We bought a *shiny red* wagon for my little brother.

Using Commas Correctly To Separate Items. Add commas where they are needed in the following sentences.

1. Linda and Nancy sent out invitations planned the menu decorated the house and waited for their guests.

2. Please write letters to Mr. and Mrs. Rogers Dr. Young and Mr. Williams.

3. The sun rose roosters crowed and the day began on the farm.

4. The campers noticed several things: first the moss on the trees; second the damp dirt; and third the broken twigs.

5. Rovers do their work quickly carefully and accurately.

6. Jenny Stone Debby Karton Liz Peterson and Moira Pease are in Ms. Mitchell's class.

7. Have you seen a dragon fly a cigar box or a cake walk?

8. We study history math science and language arts.

9. *Little Women Little House on the Prairie* and *Little House in the Big Woods* are books I've read and enjoyed.

10. First the lights went out; second thunder clapped; third I hid.

The Comma (III)

Use a comma to separate an introductory word or group of words from the rest of the sentence.

No, I don't like spinach.

Closing his eyes, Bill sat through the horror film.

The comma may be omitted if there would be little pause in speaking.

At last the game ended.

Use commas to set off words or groups of words that interrupt the flow of thought in a sentence.

This fabric, on the other hand, is pre-shrunk.

There are, I believe, three choices.

Using Commas To Set Off Words Correctly. Add commas where necessary in the following sentences. One sentence is correct.

1. Obviously we could not go in the rain.

2. The hamburger on the other hand was rare.

3. Finding himself in real danger Joe called for help.

4. Usually we go to Florida on vacation.

5. Boy is that a nice jacket!

6. Basically this story is well written.

7. My this food is disappointing.

8. Smiling widely Charlie showed us his loose tooth.

9. By the way here's the book I borrowed.

10. Yes we can fill your order.

11. Maybe I can come.

12. Unfortunately the soccer match was canceled.

13. Oh I guess so.

14. After all she is your sister.

15. That work by the way is the best I can do.

16. Everyone we were told should listen carefully.

17. There is however one condition.

18. For one thing that model car doesn't work.

19. Pointing his finger the witness identified the defendant.

20. Well we're getting ahead of our story.

The Comma (IV)

Use commas to set off nouns of direct address. A **noun of direct address** names the person to whom the speaker is speaking.

Come in, Steve, and close the door.

If the commas are omitted, the reader may be confused.

Use commas to set off most appositives. Appositives are words placed immediately after other words to make those other words clearer and more definite. Most appositives are nouns.

Mrs. Gross, my aunt, is in Florida.

When an appositive is used with modifiers, the whole group is set off with commas.

Ann, the captain of the team, is in my class.

When a noun in apposition is a first name, it is not usually set off by commas.

This is my sister Mary.

Using Commas with Nouns of Direct Address and with Appositives. Add commas where necessary in the following sentences.

1. Ms. Cavendish the insurance agent called you.

2. Dad this is my math teacher Mr. Grierson.

3. Chuckles the clown in the circus is friendly.

4. Aunt Jan I'd like you to meet my friend Millie.

5. Did you see my dog Ron?

Using Commas. Rewrite the following sentences, combining each pair into a single sentence by using a noun in apposition.

1. Dr. Tignino is our dentist. She is patient with us.

_____

2. The coach is Mr. Fisher. He is a strict man.

_____

3. The book on the shelf is *Treasure Island*. It has a leather cover.

_____

4. We visited the Art Institute. It is a beautiful building.

_____

5. Lorraine has joined the gymnastics squad. She is the new student.

_____

The Comma (V)

Use commas to set off the explanatory words of a direct quotation. Explanatory words are words like *Joyce said*, *Peter asked*, or *Fred shouted*. These words can be placed before, after, or in the middle of the exact words of the writer or speaker you are quoting.

1. Joyce said, "There is the mayor."

2. "I see him," shouted Fred.

3. "The mayor," stated Peter, "has brown hair."

When the explanatory words come before a **direct quotation,** as in the first example, the comma comes after the last explanatory word. In the second example, the explanatory words come after the direct quote, and the comma is placed after the last word of the direct quote. The third example shows the explanatory words separating the quotation. This is called a *divided quotation*, and commas are placed after the last word of the first part and after the explanatory words.

An **indirect quotation,** in which the words of the speaker are changed into your own words, uses no commas.

Joyce said that she saw the mayor.

Using Commas with Direct Quotations. Add commas wherever necessary in the following sentences. Three sentences are correct.

1. "Well" Debby sighed "the parade is over."

2. The police officer asked us to move our car.

3. "I haven't memorized that poem yet" said Joe.

4. Polly asked "Do you know Steven Haines?"

5. "Polish your shoes" suggested Mom "on the back porch."

6. "Save those trees" cautioned the ranger.

7. Dad asked us to clean the garage.

8. Mr. James asked "How many votes do I need?"

9. "Put the package down" said Len "or you'll hurt yourself."

10. "That is a great sound" said the composer.

11. Bonnie stated "I promise to tell the whole truth."

12. Bernie sang the national anthem.

13. "The weather" announced the forecaster "is cold."

14. Several people shouted "There's our home team!"

15. "Wait for us" directed Bobby "in the lobby."

The Comma (VI)

A compound sentence consists of two simple sentences joined together. **Use a comma before the conjunction that joins the two simple sentences into a compound sentence.**

The fire alarm rang, but it was only a fire drill.

The comma is not necessary in a very short compound sentence when the two simple sentences are joined by *and*.

Dorothy raced and she won.

However, always use a comma before *but* or *or*.

Dorothy raced, but she didn't win.

Do not confuse a compound sentence with a compound predicate. The two parts of a compound predicate are *not* joined by commas.

Sidney read the story and answered the questions.

Using Commas Correctly. Add commas wherever necessary in the following sentences. Watch for compound predicates.

1. The mail carrier brought the magazine but he forgot my letter.
2. I raised my head and I heard the noise.
3. Comedians tell jokes and make the audience laugh.
4. Did you see the accident or were you looking the other way?
5. Snow fell but it melted right away.
6. He has gone but he will return tomorrow.
7. The foreman liked the beginner and gave him a job.
8. Everyone in the room carefully watched the card trick but the magician fooled each of them anyway.
9. Phil studied and he passed.
10. There are eight pencils but four are broken.
11. May Linda come here or should we study at her house?
12. The twins worked together but played apart.
13. Do you know the metric system or must you learn it?
14. The boys ordered a pizza and ate it quickly.
15. Canadian pioneers moved westward and met many hardships.
16. The coyote looks like a wolf and lives in the prairies.
17. He dials the channel and he listens.
18. Diamonds are precious jewels, but they are also used in industry.
19. You may watch TV or read the newspaper for the news.
20. There were ten oil wells in the field and they all produced.

The Comma (VII)

Commas in Dates. Use commas to set off the parts of dates from each other.

> Friday,✓ October 15,✓ 1982

If a date is used in a sentence, place a comma after the last part of the date.

> November 11,✓ 1918,✓ was Armistice Day.

Commas in Locations and Addresses. Use commas between the name of a city or town and the name of its province or country.

> Trois-Rivières,✓ Quebec

Use commas to separate the parts of an address. Note that no comma is used between the province name and the postal code.

> 482 Sampler Street,✓ Moncton,✓ New Brunswick E1C 9R8

If an address is used in a sentence, place a comma after the last part.

> Please send the reply to P.O. Box 1867,✓ Stouffville,✓ Ontario L0H 1K0,✓ as requested.

Commas in Letter Parts. Use commas after the greeting of a friendly letter and after the complimentary close.

> Dear Mom,✓ Sincerely,✓

Using Commas Correctly. Add commas when necessary in the following sentences.

1. Write to 50 W. 44th Street Red Deer Alberta T4P 1Z1.

2. We're going on vacation Thursday July 5.

3. Dear Aunt Helen

4. Sir John A. Macdonald died on June 6 1891.

5. I have always wanted to live in Vancouver British Columbia.

6. Our *Maclean's* magazine was sent to Regina Saskatchewan by mistake.

7. My mom and dad's anniversary is Monday August 6.

8. Do you live in London Ontario or London England?

9. Friday July 1 we celebrate the confederation of Canada.

10. We moved from Oshawa Ontario to Brandon Manitoba.

11. Queen Elizabeth II signed Canada's Constitution Act on Saturday April 17 1982.

12. That part-time job starts Saturday December 15 and ends Saturday January 5.

13. Remember the date June 6 1944; it was D-Day.

14. We traveled from Kitchener Ontario to Lethbridge Alberta.

15. Send a card to 1185 Bendale Road Scarborough Ontario M1R 2T6 to tell us what you think.

The Semicolon and the Colon

The Semicolon. Use a **semicolon** to join the parts of a compound sentence when no coordinating conjunction is used.

> She saw the car; it was stalled.

The Colon. Use a **colon** after the greeting of a business letter.

> Dear Mr. Jones: Dear Sir or Madam:

Use a colon between numerals indicating hours and minutes.

> 4:00 P.M.

Use a colon to introduce a list of items.

> You should pack the following items: a toothbrush, two blankets, and a change of clothes.

Using Semicolons and Colons Correctly. Add the correct punctuation marks in the following sentences and phrases.

1. Five runners began the race only one finished.

2. We'll meet under the clock at Field's at 530 P.M.

3. Dear Professor

4. Bring the following things to class a pen, some paper, and an ink eraser.

5. The man tried to call home the telephone was out of order.

6. They obtained the following information about each suspect name, address, phone number, and occupation.

7. Will you be there at 900 sharp?

8. Several of the students made clocks mine was the only one that ran.

9. Our grocery list contained the following items coffee, sugar, meat, vegetables, and soda.

10. Dear Mr. Prime Minister

11. Debby wants to go to camp she chose one in Algonquin Park.

12. Throw away the paper save the card.

13. The Canucks played from 704 P.M. to 944 P.M.

14. The total came to $1.00 here is your change.

15. To make a pinwheel you need the following paper, thumbtacks, straws, pencils, and scissors.

The Hyphen

Use a hyphen to separate the parts of a word at the end of a line.

> The two boys were *begin-*
> *ning* to run.

Use a hyphen in compound numbers from *twenty-one* to *ninety-nine*. Use a hyphen in fractions.

> We need a *two-thirds* majority to pass the resolution.

Use a hyphen in such compound nouns as *great-aunt* and *commander-in-chief*.

Use a hyphen between words that make up a compound adjective used before a noun.

> Our *four-cylinder* engine is fuel efficient.

Using Hyphens Correctly. Add hyphens where necessary in the following sentences.

1. Walter Payton's number is thirty four.

2. Have you ever seen a brown eyed cat?

3. Pat wants to be a major league pitcher.

4. A three fourths majority of all provinces is necessary for the passage of the bill.

5. I gave the clerk a dollar, and I got forty five cents in change.

6. The soldier used the plane's anti aircraft gun.

7. Her gymnastics routine consisted of several flip flops, handsprings, and somersaults.

8. The boys went to the game, and in the sixth in ning they were lucky enough to catch a baseball.

9. That house is on Forty seventh Street.

10. They were divorced; she was his ex wife.

11. The recipe called for one third of a cup of milk.

12. Susan was editor in chief of the school paper.

13. All the kids liked the merry go round.

14. Some cars with eight cylinder engines were being recalled.

15. The legal driving age may be raised to twenty one.

16. She came from a well to do family.

17. I am left handed, but my brother is right handed.

18. My great grandmother is eighty one years old.

19. Mrs. Stein is a fifth grade teacher.

20. Not all sharks are man eaters.

The Apostrophe (I)

To form the possessive of a singular noun, add an apostrophe and an s.

friend + **'s** = friend's   Chris + **'s** = Chris's

To form the possessive of a plural noun that does not end in s, add an apostrophe and an s.

men + **'s** = men's   deer + **'s** = deer's

To form the possessive of a plural noun that ends in s, add only an apostrophe.

nurses + ' = nurses'   cousins + ' = cousins'

Forming the Possessives of Nouns Correctly. Write the possessive forms of the following nouns in the blanks.

1. child _____

2. Charles _____

3. robin _____

4. country _____

5. girls _____

6. fish _____

7. monkeys _____

8. dentist _____

9. cities _____

10. Ms. Klaus _____

11. game _____

12. students _____

13. priest _____

14. electrician _____

15. mice _____

16. calf _____

17. woman _____

18. pony _____

19. turkey _____

20. boys _____

21. suburbs _____

22. dog _____

23. school _____

24. women _____

25. baby _____

26. elf _____

27. presidents _____

28. secretary _____

29. carpenters _____

30. states _____

The Apostrophe (II)

Use an apostrophe in a contraction. In a contraction the apostrophe replaces one or more omitted letters.

we are → we're	cannot → can't
she is → she's	will not → won't
we will → we'll	are not → aren't

Remember, no apostrophe is used with possessive pronouns like *mine, ours, yours, his,* and *hers.*

Don't confuse these contractions with the pronouns that sound the same.

it's = it is or *it has*	*its* is the possessive of *it*
you're = you are	*your* is the possessive of *you*
they're = they are	*their* is the possessive of *they*
there's = there is	*theirs* is the possessive of *their*
who's = who is or *who has*	*whose* is the possessive of *who*

Use an apostrophe and s to form the plurals of letters, figures, and words used as words.

Ray's writing was full of *and's*.
She thinks 7's and *11's* are lucky.

Using Apostrophes Correctly. Add apostrophes wherever they are needed.

1. Well go and see the Leafs play when theyre in town.

2. Its almost time to close the store.

3. Theres nobody here; its lonely.

4. We couldnt find the battery. It wasnt in the cabinet.

5. Your ss and 5s are similar. Theyre not very neat.

Choosing the Correct Word. Underline the correct word from the two choices given in parentheses.

1. (There's, Theirs) a swallow in the birdbath.

2. Do you know (who's, whose) coat that is?

3. I (don't, dont) know if (they're, their) going to the show.

4. (It's, Its) the best thing that could happen.

5. (We'll, Well) stay for dinner if (you're, your) cooking.

Quotation Marks (I)

Use quotation marks at the beginning and at the end of a direct quotation. Quotation marks tell the reader the exact words of another speaker or writer.

Eve asked, "Can you come over after school?"

"Yes," replied Linda.

Sometimes a direct quotation is divided into two parts by explanatory words. This kind of quotation is called **a divided quotation.**

Note the placement of commas, quotation marks, and periods in the following sentences:

"I lost my notebook," moaned Larry.

Denise announced, "Dinner is ready."

"If you mow the lawn," said Kate, "I'll paint the fence."

Using Quotation Marks Correctly. Write each of the following sentences three ways as a direct quotation.

Example: The boys brought cookies.

She said, "The boys brought cookies."
"The boys," she said, "brought cookies."
"The boys brought cookies," she said.

1. I'm going to cheerleading practice at four o'clock.

_____

_____

_____

2. Jane doesn't feel well.

_____

_____

_____

3. By the way, we saw your aunt.

_____

_____

_____

Quotation Marks (II)

Place question marks and exclamation points inside quotation marks if they belong to the quotation itself.

Steve asked, "Have we ever met?"

Place question marks and exclamation points outside quotation marks if they do not belong to the quotation.

Did she say, "Help yourself"?

When you are quoting two or more sentences of a single speaker, use two sets of quotation marks if the explanatory words come in the middle.

"Mrs. Johnson called," said Gwen. "She wanted you to come to a PTA meeting Monday night. It will be about the reading program."

Only one set of quotation marks would be needed if the explanatory words come at the beginning.

Gwen said, "Mrs. Johnson called. She wanted you to come to a PTA meeting Monday night. It will be about the reading program."

In writing *dialogue* (conversation), begin a new paragraph every time the speaker changes.

"If you plan to go wandering around by yourself," she had told him, "you be mighty careful to stay out of the gully."

"Why?" Pony had asked.

Use quotation marks to set off the title of a short story, television program, poem, report, article, or chapter of a book.

Underline the title of a book, magazine, motion picture, musical composition, or painting. Underline names of ships also.

In print, these titles are set in *italics*.

Using Quotation Marks Correctly. Punctuate the following sentences, using quotation marks, end marks, underlining, and commas correctly.

1. Well asked the trainer what do you think of this horse

2. What a beauty exclaimed Josie

3. Did Josie say What a beauty

4. Stuart answered I saw him too, and he stood seventeen hands high

5. Boy would I like a horse like that sighed Melanie

6. Have you read the poem Sweet Singer by A.M. Klein?

7. John's favorite book is Born Free by Joy Adamson.

8. I always enjoy the program King of Kensington.

Review: Punctuation

Punctuating Correctly. Punctuate the following sentences correctly, using all the punctuation marks you have studied.

1. Mr Thomas J Ts father took us to the auto show on July 15

2. Wow said Joe what a treat it would be to spend all day looking around town

3. When we got there about 200 PM the parking place was three fourths filled and we had to walk around the block

4. After watching the audience applauded

5. Then Randy Sarah and Pete stayed for the second show also

6. We decided on the following items for our picnic ham sandwiches potato salad watermelon and chocolate chip cookies

7. We however couldnt decide on a restaurant

8. Yes the park pavilion will be free on the twenty ninth of June

9. We thought of going to the beach but we changed our minds when we found it was going to rain.

10. Do you always go to Ottawa Ontario in April

11. You can write to the publishing company at 471 Shuter St Montreal Quebec H3R 2B4

12. I was born December 16 1967 in Manitoba said Sheila

13. Thats quite an outfit youre wearing Ron

14. Thanks Ted Its my new suit.

15. If you write to your grandmother said Paula you'll need to write neatly. Dot your *is* and cross your *ts*.

16. I Burton Cummings
     A His music
         1 Records
         2 Concerts

17. You are old Father William the young man said
         And your hair has become very white,
     And yet you incessantly stand on your head.
         Do you think at your age it is right

18. Marcia found her glasses they were in her pocket.

19. Sandy asked us to dinner

20. What a funny ending

The Final Silent e

When a suffix beginning with a vowel is added to a word ending in silent *e*, the *e* is usually dropped.

arrange + ing = arranging   dare + ing = daring

When a suffix beginning with a consonant is added to a word ending in silent *e*, the *e* is usually retained.

hope + less = hopeless   arrange + ment = arrangement

The following words are exceptions: truly   argument   ninth   wholly

Spelling Correctly. Underline the misspelled words, and spell them correctly.

1. That was a truely frustrating experience! _____

2. Your argument was very carfully thought out. _____

3. His behaveior was unbelievable. _____

4. In my opinion that was wastful. ___ _____

5. The girl confided her fascinateing story to us. _____

6. The managment of the building was good. _____

7. Her lemonade stand was moderatly successful. _____

8. What a lovly thing to do! _____

9. Sally's dancing was gracful. _____

10. The beauty of the painting was timless. _____

11. Anne Murray is fameous. _____

12. That abbreviateion is misspelled. _____

13. That is a hopless situation. _____

14. I'm very gratful for your attention. _____

15. In the nineth inning Murcer hit a home run. _____

16. What an inviteing room! _____

17. The girl was entirly correct. _____

18. He was a great imitateor. _____

19. The carpet installers took many measurments. _____

20. Sandy had a pleaseing attitude. _____

Words Ending in y

When a suffix is added to a word ending in y preceded by a consonant, the y is usually changed to i.

family + es = families   friendly + ness = friendliness

Note the following exception: When *-ing* is added, the y does not change.

supply + ing = supplying   study + ing = studying

When a suffix is added to a word ending in y preceded by a vowel, the y usually does not change.

relay + ed = relayed   spray + ing = spraying

Adding Suffixes. Add the suffixes, and write the new word correctly.

1. happy + ness = _____

2. scurry + ing = _____

3. easy + ly = _____

4. wavy +est = _____

5. fry + ing = _____

6. forty + eth = _____

7. energy + es = _____

8. sloppy + er = _____

9. beauty + ful = _____

10. sleepy + ly = _____

11. enjoy + ment = _____

12. ally + ed = _____

13. harmony +ous = _____

14. worry + er = _____

15. body + es = _____

16. funny + est = _____

17. carry + ing = _____

18. carry + age = _____

19. try + ed = _____

20. dry + ing = _____

Adding Prefixes and Suffixes

When a prefix is added to a word, the spelling of the word remains the same.

il + legal = illegal   dis + appoint = disappoint
mis + spell = misspell   ir + responsible = irresponsible

When the suffix -ly is added to a word ending in l, both l's are retained. When -ness is added to a word ending in n, both n's are retained.

even + ness = evenness   real + ly = really
mean + ness = meanness   careful + ly = carefully

Using Prefixes and Suffixes Correctly. Underline the misspelled words, and spell them correctly.

1. Your thinking is ilogical. _____

2. Finaly, the test was done. _____

3. He is doing you a diservice. _____

4. Meaness is unacceptable. _____

5. The two candlestick holders were disimilar. _____

6. The surveyors measured the lot carefuly. _____

7. Chocolate cake is iresistible. _____

8. I met my friend accidentaly on the bus. _____

9. The reporter mistated the quotation. _____

10. She examined the plainess of the work. _____

11. Salt can be disolved in water. _____

12. They noticed the eveness of the slices. _____

13. Randy missplaced his gloves. _____

14. Santa Claus delivers presents cheerfuly. _____

15. That point is irelevant. _____

16. The gym was beautifuly decorated for the dance. _____

17. Naturaly, I forgot my notebook. _____

18. The loot was equaly divided among the pirates. _____

19. That was a terrible missadventure! _____

20. We were amazed at the thiness of the paper. _____

Words with the "Seed" Sound and Words with *ie* and *ei*

Only one English word ends in *sede: supersede.*
Three words end in *ceed: exceed, proceed, succeed.*
All other words ending in the sound of *seed* are spelled *cede:*

    concede   precede   recede   secede

When the sound is long e (ē), the word is spelled *ie* except after c.

    I BEFORE *E*: believe   niece   shield   brief
    EXCEPT AFTER *C*: receive   ceiling   perceive   conceit

The following words are exceptions:

    either   weird   species
    neither   seize   leisure

Spelling Words Correctly. Underline the misspelled words in these sentences, and spell them correctly. One sentence is correct.

    1. Neither motorist exceded the speed limit. _____

    2. The cieling had to be repaired. _____

    3. Do you think his orders will superceed yours? _____

    4. I beleive that the lawyer should concede the point. _____

    5. That theif was finally caught. _____

    6. How much mischeif can two boys get into? _____

    7. The police used a bulletproof sheild. _____

    8. Of all the decietful things to do! _____

    9. Tides receed from the shore. _____

10. Have you perceeved the fierceness of the battle? _____

11. The Stampeders yeilded the field. _____

12. A breif commercial will precede the program. _____

13. Sieze the opportunity for success. _____

14. They succeeded in entering the building. _____

15. Everyone took a liesurely walk after dinner. _____

16. Please procede with your speech. _____

17. When will you recieve your inheritance? _____

18. Susan asked the waitress for a reciept. _____

19. Was that the cheif of the Iroquois nation? _____

20. Our boat is docked at the peir. _____

Doubling the Final Consonant

Words of one syllable, ending in one consonant preceded by one vowel, double the final consonant before adding -ing, -ed, -er, or -est.

mat + ed = matted   set + ing = setting

The following words do not double the final consonant because *two* vowels precede the final consonant.

creak + ing = creaking   steal + ing = stealing

Doubling the Final Consonant. Add the suffix; then write the new word.

1. get + ing = _____

2. spin + ing = _____

3. dip + er = _____

4. pat + ed = _____

5. shut + ing = _____

6. bat + ing = _____

7. mop + ed = _____

8. moor + ing = _____

9. flip + er = _____

10. sleep + ing = _____

11. beat + er = _____

12. fret + ed = _____

13. step + ed = _____

14. drip + ing = _____

15. root + ed = _____

16. quit + er = _____

17. flop + ing = _____

18. stun + ed = _____

19. trip + ed = _____

20. trap + er = _____

21. win + ing = _____

22. wrap +ed = _____

23. soar + ed = _____

24. squeak + ing = _____

Words Often Confused (I)

accept means to agree to something or to receive something willingly.

except means to exclude or omit. As a preposition, *except* means "but" or "excluding."

affect means to influence or change.

effect is a direct result or consequence of something.

all ready expresses a complete readiness or preparedness.

already means previously or before.

des′ ert means a wilderness or dry, sandy region with sparse vegetation.

de sert′ means to abandon.

dessert is a sweet, such as cake or pie, served at the end of a meal.

hear means to listen to, or take notice of.

here means in this place.

its is a word that indicates ownership.

it's is a contraction for *it is* or *it has*.

Using Words Correctly. Underline the right word from the words in parentheses.

1. The plane had (all ready, already) left the hangar.

2. Can you (hear, hear) me over the television set?

3. Prime Ministers may not (accept, except) cash gifts.

4. (It's, Its) a sad story!

5. I never thought of (deserting, desserting); I didn't want to be disloyal.

6. Is your mood (affected, effected) by the weather?

7. Everyone (accept, except) me went to the dance.

8. My dog buried his bone (hear, hear).

9. (Desert, Dessert) is my favorite part of the meal.

10. I've been waiting for ten minutes; are you (already, all ready)?

11. Camels travel well on the (desert, dessert).

12. Did your dog lose (it's, its) collar?

13. Those cars were (accepted, excepted) from inspection.

14. The sunlight produced a dazzling (affect, effect) on the waves.

Words Often Confused (II)

lead means to go first.
led is the past tense of *lead*.
lead is a heavy, silvery-blue metal.

lose means to mislay or suffer the loss of something.
loose means free or not fastened.

past refers to that which has ended or gone by.
passed is the past tense of *pass* and means went by.

piece refers to a section or part of something.
peace means calm or quiet and freedom from disagreements or quarrels.

plane is a flat, level surface or a carpenter's tool.
plain means clearly understood, simple, or ordinary. It can also refer to an expanse of land.

principal describes something of chief or central importance. It also refers to the head of a school.
principle is a basic truth, standard, or rule of behavior.

Using Words Correctly. Underline the right word from the words in parentheses.

1. Many cars (past, passed) the accident on the expressway.

2. Use the (plain, plane) to level the door.

3. Some paint has (lead, led) in it.

4. If you (lose, loose) a tooth, put it under your pillow.

5. Have another (piece, peace) of pie.

6. The (principal, principle) of our school came on our field trip.

7. Two plus two is (plane, plain) addition.

8. Who will (lead, led) the parade?

9. In years (past, passed), we stayed up until midnight on New Year's Eve.

10. Honesty is a good (principal, principle) to live by.

11. Our neighbors said our dog's bark disturbed the (piece, peace).

12. I need to make this board smooth; hand me the (plane, plain).

13. Moses (lead, led) them to the Promised Land.

14. The handlebars on my bike are (lose, loose).

15. This article is written in (plane, plain) English.

Words Often Confused (III)

quiet refers to no noise or to something rather peaceful.
quite means really or truly, or to a considerable degree or extent.

stationary means fixed or unmoving.
stationery refers to paper and envelopes used for writing letters.

there means in that place.
their means belonging to them.
they're is a contraction for *they are*.

to means toward, or in the direction of.
too means also or very.
two is the number 2.

weather refers to atmospheric conditions such as temperature or cloudiness.
whether helps to express choice or alternative.

whose is the possessive form of *who*.
who's is a contraction for *who is*, or *who has*.

your is the possessive form of *you*.
you're is a contraction of *you are*.

Using Words Correctly. Underline the right word from the words in parentheses.

1. I ordered (stationary, stationery) with my name on it.

2. Did you walk (to, too, two) school today?

3. (Whose, Who's) there?

4. That was (quite, quiet) an exciting tennis match.

5. The horse stamped its foot (to, too, two) times.

6. Stormy (weather, whether) is due tomorrow.

7. Are these books (your, you're) books?

8. Phyllis is (there, their, they're) daughter.

9. The inspector knew (whose, who's) keys they were.

10. The door was (stationary, stationery); it wouldn't budge.

11. (Your, You're) going to the circus (to, too, two) aren't you?

12. (There, Their, They're) is Mrs. Grady, the crossing guard.

13. Teddy didn't know (weather, whether) to study or watch TV.

14. (There, Their, They're) the only survivors.

15. In a hospital, we must be (quite, quiet.)

Review: Spelling

Using Correct Spelling. Underline the misspelled words, and spell them correctly. One sentence is correct.

1. Niether the bride nor groom was ready for marriage. _____

2. We enjoyed the hospitality of those familys. _____

3. They dissapprove of the ideas of that group. _____

4. Too much worring will not solve either argument. _____

5. Carefuly, the students proceeded with the experiment. _____

6. The thiness of the ice was dangerous. _____

7. The grasshoper was lazyer than the ant. _____

8. Her niece was really grateful for the knitted scarf. _____

9. Scientists say there is a magnetic sheild around that planet. _____

10. Was Marion awfuly dissatisfied with her grade? _____

Using Words Correctly. Underline the right word from the words in parentheses.

1. That report on endangered animals has (all ready, already) been done.

2. Les stood firmly behind his (principals, principles).

3. Everyone ate (to, too, two) much at the party.

4. Nomads wander across the (desert, dessert).

5. Are you going to (accept, except) the award?

6. The shelf in the family room is (stationary, stationery).

7. What we need in this house is (piece, peace) and (quite, quiet).

8. Terry Fox has (affected, effected) millions of people.

9. Put (your, you're) homework (hear, here).

10. Our van (past, passed) all sorts of vehicles traveling west.